Cristina Bechtler &
Dora Imhof [eds.]
*The Private Museum
of the Future*

Table of Contents

PREFACE
Cristina Bechtler

Although many large public museums are based on former private collections, private museums are a phenomenon of the 20th century. Consider the Barnes Foundation in Philadelphia, the Louisiana Museum of Modern Art in Humlebæk, the Fondation Marguerite et Aimé Maeght in Saint-Paul-de-Vence, or the Judd and Chinati Foundations in Marfa. What all these institutions share is the visionary spirit of an individual. The number of such initiatives remained low for a long time, but not so today: private museums are currently springing up around the world like mushrooms. Their number is incalculable.

This book does not provide an overview; it is a selection of remarkable, exemplary individual initiatives worldwide. We put together a questionnaire on the motivations behind the foundation of private museums, and on the tasks and challenges they entail.

The answers are all very different, and what is noticeable is that many private museums no longer simply display their collections, but aim to nourish and enable art in the making.

For the successful outcome of this book I warmly thank all the authors, who took the time and effort to answer the questions. I am particularly grateful to my coeditor, Dr. Dora Imhof, for our very fruitful collaboration, and to Chris Dercon, who wrote the very insightful afterword. Many thanks also go to Katharina De Vaivre, Fredi Fischli, Philipp Kaiser, and Niels Olsen, who were on hand with help and advice.

My thanks also go to Patricia Mosquera, who always kept the overview, and to Clément Dirié of JRP|Ringier for his continuous support.

Introduction
Dora Imhof

Worldwide museums of contemporary art continue to be founded, and existing ones are expanding. Almost every day conferences are held in which museum-related topics are discussed: architecture, art education, digitalization, globalization, diversity, display, and storage. And in the past few years numerous books have been published dedicated to museums. This includes our own book *Museum of the Future*, first published in 2014 and reprinted this year.[1]

Among this current museum boom one trend is particularly manifest: the proliferation of private museums. In the spring and fall of 2017 the Marciano Art Foundation in Los Angeles and the Zeitz MOCAA–Museum of Contemporary Art Africa in Cape Town opened their doors. Artists like Thomas Schütte, Hiroshi Sugimoto, and Yayoi Kusama are creating their own museums, and two of the most talked about exhibitions at the Venice Biennale 2017 took place at the Fondazione Prada and the two Venice-venues of the French mega collector François Pinault.

These private initiatives are viewed with fascination by some and greeted with criticism by others—or a combination of both. However, in contrast to the vast literature dedicated to every aspect of museums, private museums are still a blind spot that has remained largely unexplored and has not been analyzed in depth. Only slowly are documentation and research beginning to catch up: the book *Kunstsammlerinnen. Peggy Guggenheim bis Ingvild Goetz*, published in 2009, focused on female collectors, several of whom were also museum founders.[2] The architecture of private museums and public private partnerships have been discussed in academic publications.[3] In fall 2017 a conference dedicated to private museums took place at the Technical University in Berlin.[4] Already in the summer of that year Cristina Bechtler, Katharina De Vaivre, and Christopher Noe had organized the first Private Museum Conference in Basel. In addition, several surveys have also begun to document the rise of the private museum. The *Private Art Museum Report*, published in 2015 by Larry's List, counted 317 privately founded contemporary art museums.[5] This "first global study," in which over 160 museums participated, contained many interesting findings, such as the strong presence of private museums in Asia, particulary in South Korea, and that museum founders tend to be male and around 60 years old. Another survey is *The BMW Art Guide by Independent Collectors*. The first issue compiled in 2012 contained over 160 publicly accessible private collections; the second, published in 2013, listed 217 art collections, and the third and last counted 236 in 2015.[6] Numbers quickly become obsolete, as the private museum world is very dynamic; new institutions are being founded while others close their doors forever—numbers and statistics, as relevant as they are, only tell part of the story and little of the history of private museums and their founders.

Some of the motivations of private collectors and museum founders were addressed in our book *Museum of the Future* where, alongside interviews with artists, architects, curators, and museum directors, we asked all the participants about the role of private collectors in the art world. The book also contained interviews with the private collectors Nicoletta Fiorucci, Maja Hoffmann, and Julia Stoschek. We considered the recent developments to be so interesting and significant that we decided to make a second book dedicated exclusively to private museums.

Histories and Geographies

Private museums dedicated to contemporary art are not a new phenomenon. The United States in particular have a vital tradition of private museums. As early as 1920, the artist, collector, and mediator Katherine S. Dreier, and the artists Marcel Duchamp and Man Ray founded the Société Anonyme Inc., which defined itself as a private museum and organized the *International Exhibition of Modern Art* at the Brooklyn Museum in 1926–1927, among many other exhibitions. The Phillips Collection in Washington DC was founded by Duncan and Marjorie Phillips in 1921 as the first modern art museum in the United States. The Solomon R. Guggenheim Museum in New York opened its doors in 1939. Peggy Guggenheim's space Art of The Century in Manhattan followed in 1942 and was both a gallery and a museum. In 1974 Philippa de Menil and Heiner Friedrich founded the Dia Art Foundation, and the Menil Collection in Houston opened its doors in 1987, to name just a few of the most renowned institutions.

In Europe there are other eminent examples. In 1913, the German collector Helene Kröller-Müller founded a private museum in The Hague—later she donated her collection to the state and it developed into the now-public Kröller-Müller Museum in Otterlo. In Łódź, Poland, the artists' group a.r. began collecting avant-garde works in 1929 for a museum that was to open in 1931: the Muzeum Sztuki w Łodzi, as it is called today, became state-owned in 1950. The Louisiana Museum of Modern Art in Humlebæk near Copenhagen, which several interviewees in *Museum of the Future* named as their favorite museum, was initiated by Knud W. Jensen in 1958; and the famous and much-loved Fondation Maeght in Saint-Paul-de-Vence opened its doors in 1964.

In some respects the motivations of today's museum founders are comparable to those of their predecessors:

a passion for collecting contemporary art combined with the passion for sharing it with a broader public. The wish to create a unique site, often combined with exceptional architecture, and the desire to keep a collection as a whole. Still, the situation today is different: in contrast to the greater part of the 20th century, contemporary art is now widely accepted, and an integral part of public collections. Both the art world, and in particular the art market, have grown and changed beyond recognition. It is crucial also to situate the private museum boom in this contemporary context.

With recent changes, power relations in the art world have shifted. Private collectors have always been privileged because of the freedom and flexibility private means allow—but let us also not forget that besides the super rich collectors who attract so much attention today, there are many others that have made and still make things possible with comparatively small means, and who undertake considerable commitments and risks with their enterprises. Now that prices for contemporary art have reached previously unimaginable heights while the means of public collections have not grown in equal measure or are even under threat, the power of private collectors is perceived as particularly strong. In his book *Siegerkunst*, the German art historian Wolfgang Ullrich deplored that art has become mainly a status symbol for the wealthy, in which prices and names get much more attention than (critical) content.[7]

Let us also not forget that with the growth and expansion of the art world and with globalization, private museums for contemporary art are no longer a North American or European phenomenon. Together with history, geography is a central factor. For many reasons, a private museum in China, Korea, or Lebanon is very different to a private museum in Switzerland or the United States—as Chris Dercon discusses in the afterword of this volume. Where there are few public institutions and very limited or one-sided political support for the arts, for instance, private collectors and museums can have an essential role in supporting an art scene, preserving its heritage, and making visible a broader perspective.

The Swiss Scene

The situation in Switzerland—our own background—is in itself very interesting and diverse, and each private endeavor is unique in its own way. Switzerland has a vital museum scene and tradition in which private and public engagements are often intertwined. The nucleus of the public Kunstmuseum Basel is a private collection: the Amerbach Cabinet acquired by the city in 1661. The beginnings of the Kunsthaus Zürich go back to the collecting activities of a society of artists. The collector Oskar Reinhart initated a museum in Winterthur that after his death became state-owned. Today the situation is still dynamic: the Kunsthaus Zürich is building an extension that will also make room for the E. G. Bührle Collection. In contrast, Hallen für Neue Kunst in Schaffhausen, founded by Urs and Christel Raussmüller in 1984, which became an influential model for museums of contemporary art all over the world, closed in 2014.

The most successful Swiss museum today in terms of annual visitors is the Fondation Beyeler in Riehen, founded in 1997. Before the foundation of his museum, the art dealer Ernst Beyeler had been in discussion with the Kunstmuseum Basel for many years about the placing of his collection in the museum.[8] In the end Ernst and Hildy Beyeler decided to build their own museum designed by Renzo Piano that has continued to thrive after the death of the founders; an extension is currently being built with Peter Zumthor. There are new additions to the Swiss Scene, such as the Muzeum Susch in Zernez in the region of Engadin, by Polish collector Grażyna Kulczyk, and a large complex in Männedorf near Zurich designed by Baier Bischofberger architects for the Bruno Bischofberger collection, open for the time being only by appointment.

Not all Swiss private collectors build museums: Uli Sigg donated his vast collection of Chinese Art to M+ in Hong Kong. In addition there are successful, time-tested public-private collaborations and the search for new forms of display and reseach. The collection of the Emanuel Hoffmann Foundation, directed today by Maja Oeri, can be visited in the innovative storage and museum space Schaulager in Münchenstein, founded by the Laurenz Foundation and opened in 2003, but also in part at the

Kunstmuseum Basel. This close connection between the Emanuel Hoffmann Foundation and the public art museum was established in 1936 by Oeri's grandmother Maja Sacher.[9] In 2002 and 2013 the Laurenz professorship and the Schaulager professorship for contemporary art and art theory were established at the University of Basel.

Maja Hoffmann's LUMA foundation has founded an exhibition space next to the Kunsthalle Zürich in the Löwenbräu building. In Arles in the South of France the LUMA foundation is developing an ambitious interdiciplinary center dedicated to research, archives, and education with a 55-meter tower designed by Frank Gehry in the Parc des Ateliers.

Criticisms, Tankers, and Speedboats

Not all initiatives by private museum founders are unanimously welcomed. They have been criticized as being either too spectacular and ego-driven, or too mainstream in their collecting policies. Criticism can be both locally-oriented or global. Usually large-scale projects receive the brunt of the criticism: locals, neighboring institutions, politicians, and artists attack projects deemed too overpowering, elitist, or politically suspect. Sometimes successfully: when he wanted to build a museum in Zurich designed by Rem Koolhaas in the early 2000s, German collector Friedrich Christian Flick was so heavily criticized that he moved his collection to Berlin instead.

The global, general critique of private museums is directed toward power shifts and the heightened importance of money in the artworld, or capitalist critique, *tout court*.[10] Sometimes, or often, local and general critique are mixed.

The important role that private collectors exert in the art and museum world is, however, uncontested. In our book *Museum of the Future*, all interviewees underscored the vital importance of private collectors for museums: as donors, board members, partners, engaged visitors, and constructive critics. The economists Nathalie Moureau, Dominique Sagot-Duvauroux, and Marion Vidal also examined the role of collectors of contemporary art in France, without, however, mentioning private museums.[11]

It has been stressed that private collectors can be more radical, experimental, and faster in their collecting than public institutions where decisions have to be agreed on by boards and committees and are made under the eyes of the public and politicians. They can also look at the otherwise overlooked, explore unique, even idiosyncratic paths. Collectors who aim beyond mainstream or consensus taste can be the speedboats to the tankers or the cruiseships that are public institutions, or pioneers in testing new forms of institutions.

When collectors build private museums the stakes are different: naturally public museums would rather incorporate an attractive private collection than have an attractive new private museum next door as competition.[12] But since today's art world is huge and the storage spaces of museums and private collectors are equally full is it not preferable that a private collector found a museum open to the public and not leave the works in their homes where only a few people can see them, or in storage spaces and free ports inaccessible to the public? Collectors not only build museums as vehicles to save taxes or as displays of wealth and taste, but also because they prefer independence, or have very individual ideas about art and its display.[13]

Two questions remain central though. One concerns power. As private individuals, collectors and museum founders are free to spend their own money as they choose. If this concerns great wealth this involves considerable power and agency, as David Callahan has discussed in *The Givers: Money, Power, and Philanthropy in a New Gilded Age*.[14] Because of the impact of their decisions, mega collectors and mega donors have responsibilities. When art history is written from above by wealthy individuals this has effects on the canon. The conditions of gifts, and the specifics of private public partnership must be made transparent.[15]

The other problem is the long-term sustainability of these initiatives. Chris Dercon makes trenchant observations regarding this topic in the afterword to this publication. But since some of the oldest museums in the world started as private collections, the future does not look too bleak.

New Models?

So what might these new ideas and forms for private museums be? If we look at the examples in this book, there is no simple answer to the question "What is a private art museum?" There are a multitude of approaches. In the spring of 2017 we sent the questionnaire to almost 50 institutions/collectors we found most relevant or interesting to answer or rather assess this question, as they have undertaken, for a long time or more recently, innovative private initiatives for collecting, showing, and/or producing contemporary art. It was important for us to cover a wide range of museums, big and small, on different continents. Many were happy to join the dialogue. Interestingly, American-based institutions—a country where private collectors are particularly important agents in the museum world—were rather reluctant to participate.

Our publication with 24 collectors can offer only a very small glimpse into the recent developments, but hopefully it will enliven the discussion about what a private art museum is or could be. Several tendencies became manifest: many collectors aim to transcend the concept of the museum as a monolitic building. They consciously avoid the term "museum," like the Samdani Art Foundation in Bangladesh. Some adopt the model of the Kunsthalle, for example the Fondazione Sandretto Re Rebaudengo in Turin and Madrid, and the Parasol unit foundation for contemporary art in London. Or they may have no fixed premises and collaborate with different institutions and initatives, such as the itinerant NEON foundation in Athens, or they may work as initiatives for sharing, studying, and preserving art, like the Saradar Collection in Lebanon.

Other collectors are developing new forms of institutions as centers for research and production, like Maja Hoffmann in Arles. Others are happy to adopt the classic museum model, like the Goetz Collection in Munich, founded as one of the first private museums in 1993—part of the Goetz Collection was donated to the Free State of Bavaria in 2004.

Museums are mainly situated in cities. But a notable number of private initatives seek a close connection within the natural environment—in particular the Benesse Art Site

Naoshima in Japan; Instituto Inhotim in Brazil, and Lu Xun's Sifang Art Museum in Nanjing in China. Philippe Méaille in the Loire Valley and Bernar Venet in Le Muy, both in France, and David Walsh's Museum of Old and New Art in Hobart, Tasmania, are also relevant here. Now that the focus is so much on the private enterprises of mega collectors and designs by starchitects, it is also important to stress that many museums are small and intimate. It is maybe exactly this diversity, and the will to experiment that will be most inspiring.

[1] Cristina Bechtler and Dora Imhof (eds.), *Museum of the Future*, JRP | Ringier, Zurich 2014; reprinted in 2018.

[2] Dorothee Wimmer, Christina Feilchenfeldt, Stephanie Tasch (eds.), *Kunstsammlerinnen. Peggy Guggenheim bis Ingvild Goetz*, Reimer, Berlin 2009.

[3] Craig Buckley, Mark Wasiuta (eds.), *Collecting Architecture Territories*, Columbia University's Graduate School of Architecture Planning and Preservation and Deste Foundation for Contemporary Art, New York 2014; Katrin Louise Holzmann, *Sammler und Museen. Kooperationsformen der Einbindung von privaten zeitgenössischen Kunstsammlungen in die deutsche Museumslandschaft*, Springer, Wiesbaden 2016.

[4] *The Global Power of Private Museums: Arts and Publics—States and Markets*, Centre for Art Market Studies, Technische Universität, Berlin, November 16–18, 2017.

[5] Larry's List, AMMA (eds.), *Private Art Museum Report*, 2015, www.larryslist.com/report/Private%20Art%20Museum%20 Report.pdf (last accessed May 2018).

[6] *The BMW Art Guide*, BMW Group/Independent Collectors, Berlin 2012, 2013, 2015.

[7] Wolfgang Ullrich, *Siegerkunst. Neuer Adel, teure Lust*, Klaus Wagenbach Verlag, Berlin 2016.

[8] Martin Schwander, "Die Sammlung Beyeler. Ein Gespräch mit dem Kunsthändler Ernst Beyeler über den zukünftigen Standort seiner Sammlung," in *z'Rieche. Ein heimatliches Jahrbuch*, Riehen 1991, p. 114–121.

[9] Susanne Kudielka, "Eine Stiftung für noch nicht allgemein verstandene Ausdrucksmittel. Die Sammlerin Maja Sacher," in *Kunstsammlerinnen*, p. 180.

[10] See for instance www.theatlantic.com/entertainment/ archive/2015/09/at-the-broad-museum-the-architecture-rivals-the-art/404584/ (last accessed May 2018). Etienne Dumont, "Arles/La mécène Maja Hoffmann est-elle devenue vraiment omnipotente?" *Bilan*, July 28, 2016. http://www.bilan.ch/etienne-dumont/courants-dart/ arlesla-mecene-maja-hoffmann-vraiment-devenue-omnipotente (last accessed May 2018). For a general critique, see Wolfgang Ullrich, *Siegerkunst*, and Luc Boltanski and Arnaud Esquerre, *Enrichissement: Une critique de la marchandise*, Gallimard, Paris 2017.

[11] Nathalie Moureau, Dominique Sagot-Duvauroux, Marion Vidal, "Collectionneurs d'art contemporain : des acteurs méconnus de la vie artistique," in *Cultures études*, 1/2015, p. 1–20, Paris.

[12] An article in *Le Monde* discusses the effect of the Fondation Louis Vuitton, founded by Bernard Arnault in Paris: www.lemonde.fr/arts/article/2016/10/28/ bernard-arnault-fait-peur-aux-musees_5021774_1655012. html (last accessed May 2018).

[13] See www.nytimes.com/2015/01/11/business/art-collectors-gain-tax-benefits-from-private-museums.html (last accessed May 2018).

[14] David Callahan, *The Givers: Money, Power and Philanthropy in a New Gilded Age*, Knopf, New York 2017. See also Andrea Fraser and Eric Golo Stone, "Philanthropy and Plutocracy," in *October*, Fall 2017, no. 162, p. 31–38.

[15] These two points were also stressed at the 2017 conference in Berlin; the term "art history from above" I take from Kathryn Brown's talk (see footnote 4).

Ziba Ardalan
Parasol unit foundation for contemporary art, London

Dr. Ziba Ardalan is the founder, director, and curator of Parasol unit foundation for contemporary art, an educational charity and nonprofit exhibition space in London. She has curated numerous exhibitions of contemporary art, almost 50 of which have taken place at Parasol unit. Prior to her career in art, Ardalan obtained a PhD in Physical Chemistry.

Year of foundation: 2004
Size: n/a
Number of employees: 8 (office staff)
Number of visitors: c. 50,000 (2016)

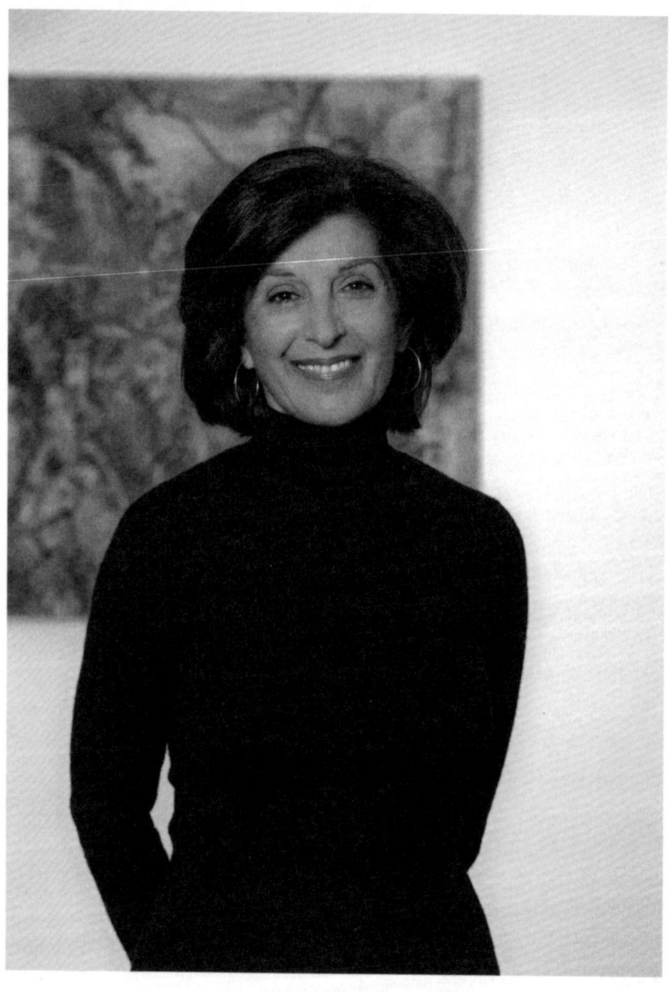

What was your main motivation in founding a museum?

I was a born curator I assume, even though, due to the time and my circumstances, I first studied for a PhD in Physical Chemistry and only later, in 1980, followed up with additional studies in the history of art and professional experience working in contemporary art. Therefore, the activity of curating art exhibitions has far more relevance in my life than anything else I could possibly have done in the field of art. In 2004 when I set up Parasol unit, I was determined to hold high quality exhibitions of international art and forgo altogether the pursuit of collecting. The motivation to do so was, on the one hand, to avoid any conflict of interest, and on the other to have total freedom and full objectivity in conceiving and organizing temporary exhibitions.

Did you have a specific model (i.e. an existing collection) in mind, and is there a tradition in your family of collecting art?

Parasol unit was founded on the model of the continental European Kunsthalle, which literally means a hall for art. One commonly comes across such spaces in Swiss and German towns, and we know that, unlike museums, Kunsthallen do not have a permanent collection. Rather, what they do have is the freedom to stage contemporary art exhibitions—whatever the word "contemporary" means at any given time.

Since my student days in Switzerland, I have been fascinated by the Kunsthalle model, and the economy of means by which they are run. I remember how surprised I was in the 1970s to learn that these critically important art institutions with their often vibrant and ambitious exhibition programs were essentially run by just four staff members. Indeed, and as I said earlier, the fact of being without a permanent collection offered them unparalleled freedom to think purely in terms of the art of the time and their exhibition. Not having a private collection was fundamental to my philosophy for Parasol unit. I also have to admit that as a whole I am not a gatherer.

As to whether there was a tradition of collecting in my family, of course any established Persian family used to have some kind of collection. It remains to be seen whether collecting is a physical act of assembling objects or, rather, a conceptual one.

What is the focus of your collection? Do you focus on the presentation of your collection or on organizing temporary exhibitions?

Parasol unit presents only temporary art exhibitions to show the work of artists from around the world.

How did you choose the location of the museum?

I set up Parasol unit in 2004, during a glorious period in the history of contemporary art in London. Four years previously, Tate Modern had opened its doors to the public and dramatically changed the range and significance of international contemporary art here.

Having embarked on a career in art in 1980 when
I moved to New York City, which I had also visited during
the 1970s, I was familiar with SoHo when that area of the
city predominantly housed artists' studios, lofts, and art
galleries, without the distraction of today's fashion boutiques
and posh restaurants. Post-World War II, artists required the
kind of neutral, vast, and almost rough working spaces that
warehouses could offer. So, my own concept of presenting
contemporary artworks was pretty much formed during this
period in New York.

Once in London, and about to open Parasol unit,
I looked nowhere for a gallery space other than in East
London. I enjoyed the unpretentious quality of the neighborhood and the total absence of the distractions present
in more fashionable places, even though that meant it was
difficult to find a decent restaurant for lunch. In 2004,
this area of Hackney near the Old Street roundabout was
still affordable for artists and students to live and work in.
I loved the uncanny nature of the neighborhood. This has
been changed dramatically by all these new buildings that
have gone up subsequently in the vicinity of the foundation,
but on the positive side they have increased the audience
for our exhibitions and events.

Parasol unit is housed in a former Victorian furniture
factory, where the souls of countless workers, who worked
endless hours here, are still felt today. In fact, whenever
I invite an artist to exhibit at the foundation, they are won
over by the spirit of the place. We do not have enormous
gallery spaces or extremely high ceilings, but there is
something special about the spirit of human endeavor here
that resonates with artists, staff members, and visitors alike.
The space also benefits from natural light and is remarkably
flexible, which means it can be modified to accommodate
the needs of each exhibition.

How did you choose the architect?

When we decided to refurbish the space, we selected the
Italian architect Claudio Silvestrin. He is well known for his
minimalist approach and clean lines in architecture and, as
expected, he quickly came up with an elegant and reductive
design that integrated most of the columns that were

crowding the space. With the heating and air-conditioning cleverly hidden within the architecture, our two floors of gallery space are maximized to provide plenty of room for a mid-career survey exhibition, or for a focused and curated presentation of works by an established artist. We back onto the Wenlock Basin section of Regent's Canal and the beautiful greenery surrounding it, and this provides us with a delightful exterior space, which allows us to accommodate outdoor sculptures and various installations on our terrace.

For example, as part of our wider projects, once a year we commission a different artist to create an outdoor work that addresses the phenomenon of light. The resulting Parasol*stice*-Winter Light series adds a special touch to our exhibition program throughout the short, dark days of winter. Also, if required, our versatile education room can provide additional exhibition space, as it did in the autumn of 2017 when we used it to present a selection of works on paper as part of the splendid exhibition we dedicated to Martin Puryear.

How strongly are you involved in the running of the museum (programming, management, etc.)?

As I said earlier, I am a born curator, so starting and running Parasol unit would never have happened with anything less than my full involvement as curator and director of the space. Like anything one undertakes and wants to make a success of, for the first six or seven years I worked at 500% capacity without having really foreseen that it would be this way.

Do you have an education program?

Indeed, Parasol unit has an important and innovative education program for adults, children, and families. The adult education program is very much based on our changing exhibitions and other projects. It includes panel discussions, gallery talks, poetry, and tailor-made workshops.

The education program for families and children has several strands and we continually revisit and develop the concept. Currently, the four strands of the family education program include: Sunday workshops; school visits, scheduled

by appointment, which entail a visit to the current exhibition
followed by a workshop for an entire class; our Early Years
program aimed at children below the age of five; and a Youth
Program, which usually runs over three days during half-
term breaks. Since 2016, we have also hosted the annual
two-day London Children's Book Fair.

What is your relationship with public and other institutions?
Do you receive (public or private) funding?

Through its clear mission statement, Parasol unit was able,
early on, to distinguish itself as an institution on a par with
any other nonprofit organization. Of course, the fact that
the foundation does not collect art helps tremendously to
avoid any potential conflict of interest. These circumstances
have allowed the foundation to receive project-based public
funding as well as funding from charitable organizations.

    The foundation is located in the Borough of
Hackney, but the other side of Wharf Road is in the Borough
of Islington. So the foundation serves both boroughs as
well as other boroughs of London. Engaging with the various
communities that surround us has made Parasol unit an
increasingly vibrant institution and added a local level of
dialogue to its otherwise international exhibition program.

    As for collaborating with other institutions, we
sometimes do so in our education program, but of course
one could always do more. Some years ago, the Whitechapel
Gallery and Parasol unit initiated First Thursdays, which
coordinated more than 150 East End institutions and
commercial galleries to remain open late on the first
Thursday of each month. More recently, Parasol unit has
embarked on organizing another wonderful initiative known
as the East End Gallery Trail, which brings a visible geo-
graphical unity to the institutions and commercial galleries
of the East End. There is now a comprehensive map, and
other related projects are underway, all of which shows what
a significant body we are in this part of London, and how
we benefit our local inhabitants and communities. On the
whole, London cultural institutions are extremely active and
busy with their own program. This often means that institutions do not have enough time to think of collaborating,
but it does provide the public with numerous and disparate

exhibitions and the opportunity to participate in countless events.

In the past five years, what has been your greatest joy in running the museum? And what has been the biggest challenge?

Ever since Parasol unit opened in 2004, every day of its existence has been a joy and, at times, a challenge. I don't think it is possible to separate those two feelings while one is responsible for the complex task of running such an institution. During the past five years at Parasol unit, one of the most important events was without doubt the 10th anniversary auction and celebration. Countless artists, whether or not they had exhibited at the foundation, generously donated artworks for the auction. Aside from the significant amount of almost £2.5 million raised by the auction, it demonstrated the level of friendship and appreciation that the artists felt toward the foundation. For me, this expression of friendship was far more rewarding and significant than any sum we raised.

As I have already said, joy has been mixed with challenge in whatever I have done at Parasol unit. When I started the foundation, I did it purely out of my love for art and a sense of responsibility, a need to give something back to society. I had little idea of what it would entail to found and run an institution that presents four high quality curated exhibitions a year, each with an accompanying publication, alongside other artistic projects and a full education program. I did not really know yet how much of a perfectionist I am, and therefore did not realize the magnitude of the effort that would be required. Also, I started Parasol unit in a city that was already extraordinarily rich in museums and culture, and I knew practically no one in the art world.

It is impossible to talk about the pleasure and challenges of any particular project, because the reason I decided to do them was that imagining the work of any one of the artists in my gallery space simply filled me with joy. Each exhibition or project has its own unique challenges and the reason I am still working at Parasol unit, after almost 14 years, is that I am addicted to this joy and challenge.

*What can a private museum do, that public institutions cannot? How do
you respond to people who criticize the proliferation of private museums?*

Privately funded museums that have a collecting arm
and organize exhibitions, including works from their own
collection, may well come under criticism from some
members of the public. However, most owners of a private
collection are far better intentioned than their detractors.
We live in prosperous times and it is far better to exhibit
wonderful works of art for the public to view than to keep
them in storage. I am definitely a positive person and look
for solutions rather than scrutinizing people's negative
reactions. In any case, building a museum and supporting it
financially is a sign of generosity. It is my hope, if I may say
so, that every such museum has an endowment sufficient
to take care of its collection forever.
     At Parasol unit, I intentionally opted to present only
temporary exhibitions, which allows me to continue the
undertaking for as long as I find it beneficial or helpful.
I once read an intelligent comment by the American critic
and philosopher Arthur Danto who said, "The art museum
as an institution is only 200 years old. There's no reason
why it has to go on forever. It's not like a hospital, after all."[1]
I think herein lies the advantage and flexibility of private
museums or institutions. Such organizations should serve
some defined need and hopefully inspire others to do
something similar, but different.
     Private museums also benefit from being relatively
small in size, and therefore have certain freedoms and
the flexibility to act faster than state-run museums.

*What are the greatest challenges in the long-term development of
a private museum? And what are your plans for the next generation?*

I would say that the most significant challenge is to run an
institution at the highest level, year in and year out, and to
prepare it for the future if we decide it has to have a future.
No one has been able to control life after they have left
the world, therefore the best we can do is to pass on a love
of art to our children, leave a hefty endowment to run the
institution, and hope for the best. My own instinct is to give
them a love of art and let them decide.

Do you have any unrealized projects?

Of course, people with an entrepreneurial spirit never stop.
Since 2004, when I started Parasol unit, there has been
a new addition to our program every other year, at least.
One thing I would not want to do though is to double
the footprint of the institution. I love the curatorial work
and the contact with artists, therefore embarking on any
extra fundraising or building project now would distract me
from what I love most, which is the art.

Do you have any unrealized projects?

[1]   William Grimes, "Three Specialists Check the Vital Signs
      of the Art Museum," *The New York Times*, February 15, 1994.
      https://www.nytimes.com/1994/02/15/arts/three-specialists-
      check-the-vital-signs-of-the-art-museum.html
      (last accessed May 2018).

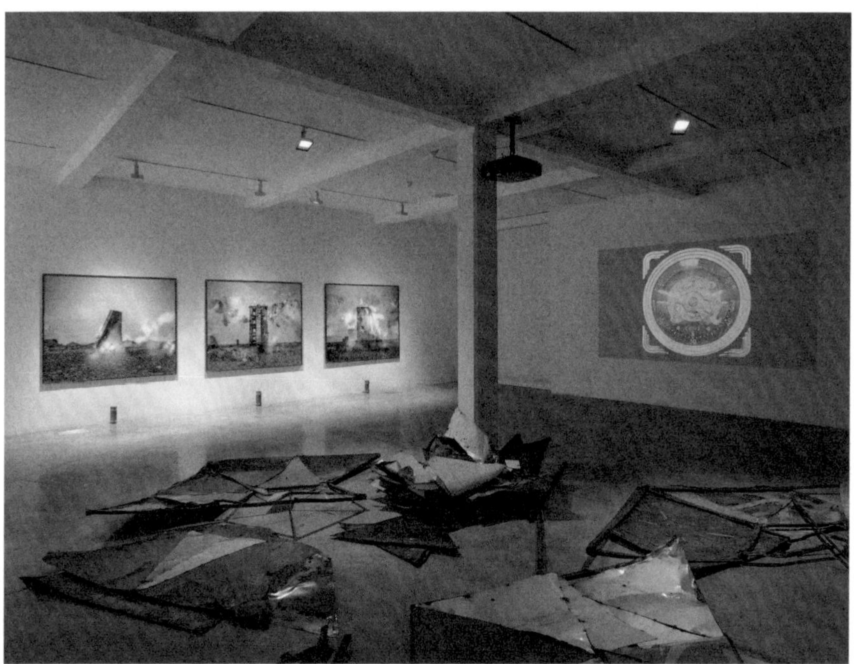

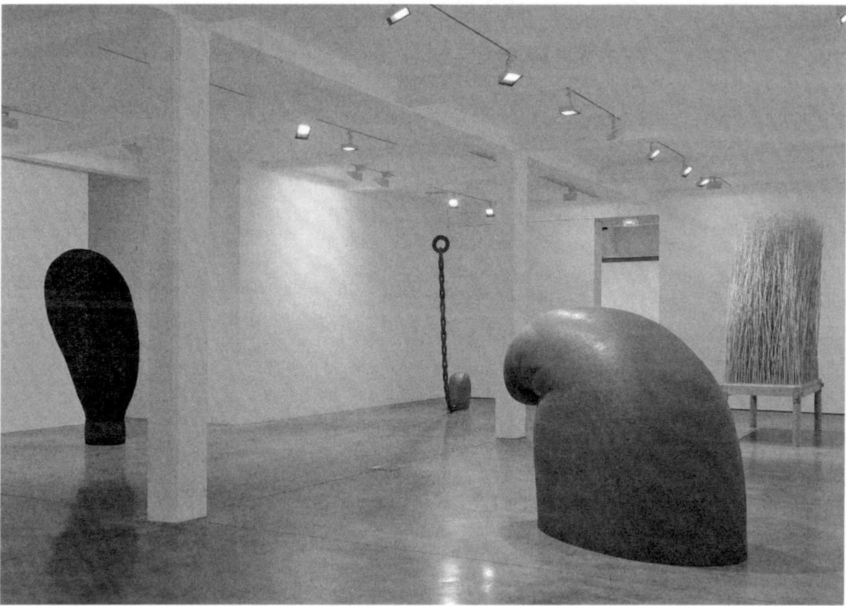

View of the exhibition *Julian Charrière*, Parasol unit foundation for contemporary art, London, 2016
View of the exhibition *Martin Puryear*, Parasol unit foundation for contemporary art, London, 2017

Christian Boros
Boros Collection, Berlin

Christian Boros is a media entrepreneur and art collector. In 1990 he founded the Boros –
Agentur für Kommunikation, and in 2010 he cofounded the publishing company Distanz,
both based in Berlin.

Year of foundation: 2008
Size: 3,000 m^2
Employees: c. 26
Visitors: 120,000 (2008–2012), 200,000 (2012–2016)

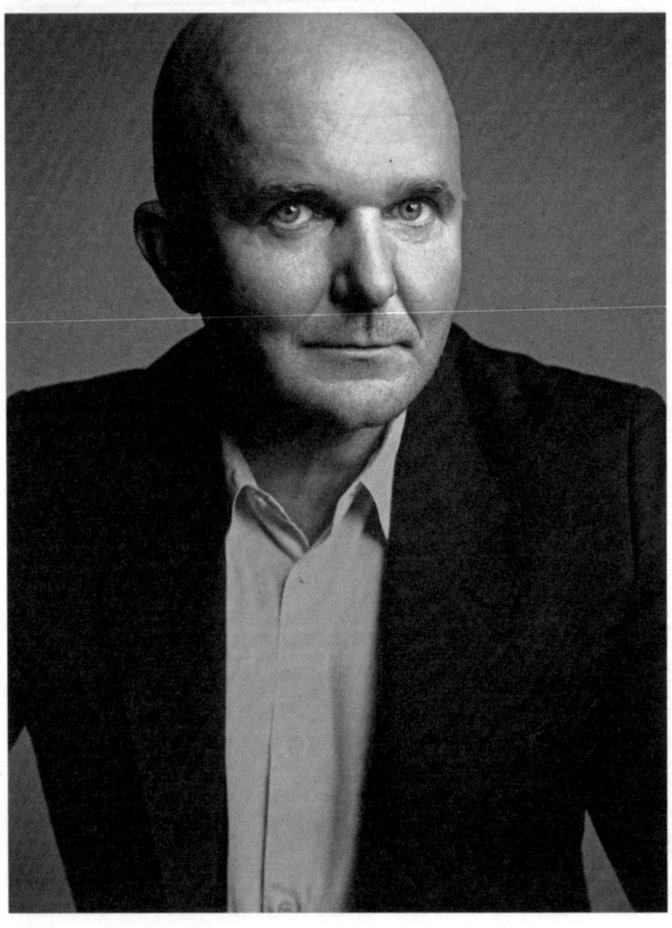

*What was your main motivation
in founding a museum?*

First of all we should define what
exactly is understood as a private
museum. We run a collection that
is neither a museum nor a private
museum. I see us as a private space
that can be visited by appointment, and that shows fragments of
our collection. A museum has very
different tasks.
     After having collected for
20 years, we realized that artists do
not create works in order to have
them just stored in wooden crates.
Art wants to be exhibited, to be
seen, and we wanted to share our
collection of works with the public.

*Did you have a specific model in mind,
and is there a tradition in your family
of collecting art?*

There is not such a thing as
a family tradition, but Erika
Hoffmann's private collection was
a huge role model. My wife Karen

and I especially admired the art mediation she offered along with the visit to her exhibitions. Contemporary art becomes understandable and accessible for any visitor when you not only walk past the works and look at them, but when it is talked about. It was clear from the beginning that we wanted to offer these communicational bridges toward an understanding of art through art mediators in our collection too.

What is the focus of your collection? Do you focus on the presentation of the collection or on organizing temporary exhibitions?

We do not organize exhibitions, but show works from our collection. The focus really lies on contemporary art in any medium. We collect internationally. Each presentation contains mostly works that have just been produced.

How did you choose the location of the museum?

From the beginning Karen and I looked out for unexceptional places with historical references. We definitely did not want a new construction, but rather a place that would gain a new meaning, a new function on being transformed into a private collection space. Other than that we were completely open to ideas. We actually looked at a lot of different possible venues—around the year 2000 there were still a lot of properties of that sort on the market—but the moment we found out about the bunker it was clear we had found the right place. The building had been on the market for more than two years and was screaming for help.

How did you choose the architect?

In a quite unusual way: we googled him. We actually just wanted to find out about the general history of bunkers in Berlin, and Jens Casper appeared in the search results because he had been involved with our bunker before. We wanted to meet him to just get some information, but then we fell in love with his vision for converting the bunker so we choose him as the architect for both the old part and the new part on top of the building—our penthouse. He had never built anything previously.

How strongly involved are you in the running of the museum?

We are a team of around 26 people and one director, Juliet Kothe. My wife and I decide what enters the collection, but the rest—the mediation program, the team leading the coordination of it all—lies in the hands of the director and her team.

Do you have an educational program?

The core of the visit is the art mediation—every visitor participates in a 90 minute guided tour. There are no exceptions: every visit somehow is also educational.

What is your relationship with public and other institutions? Do you get public or private funding?

Everything is private. We receive neither private nor governmental funding. The relationship to other institutions I regard as good, sometimes even friendly—whether they are private or not.

In the past five years what has been your greatest joy? And your biggest challenge?

I was incredibly happy when I found out that more than 200,000 people from all over the world had visited our last presentation. It is an enormous number, especially considering that we only offer tours with 12 people at a time. It makes me so very happy to have people interested in what we are interested in.
     The new presentation is really a challenge. To curate an exhibition together with the artists that makes sense in these spatial circumstances that have not been constructed for exhibiting art is difficult.

What can a private institution do, that public institutions cannot? How do you respond to people who critize the profileration of private museums?

You feel the subjectivity of the collectors in a private collection. In that sense public museums are much more neutral, objective, and complete in their representation of art. We have up to 50 works by certain artists in our collection—although ten works would have been enough in order to represent the artist in an adequate way. If we admire an artist we allow ourselves to substantially collect a body of work, and therefore other artists who might be equally relevant to the artistic expression of a certain time (but not for us) can't be included.

This kind of subjective selection, and also the way we can choose how and what we present represents an enormous freedom. Our visitors appreciate this subjectiveness—and hopefully they are aware that the outcome of our engagement results from a passion, not a job.

What are the greatest challenges in the long-term development of a private museum? And what are your plans for the next generation?

The most tremendous advantage really is that you can be brave and quick in the support and collecting of an artist, whereas museums are not that flexible financially. They often have to be patient in order to collect the money and to find supporters to purchase a work.

What is still a big challenge is the polarization between public museums and private collections. It is a challenge sometimes to come to an agreement with each other. Both sides of the art world—private and public—will continue to exist. They should be thinking of each other as collaborators, not as the "other." Especially in a city like Berlin, where the number of private institutions is still growing, it should be a duty to work together in a symbiotic, pleasant, reasonable, and collaborative manner.

Do you have unrealized projects?

So many that I don't even know where to start. With each work, with each artist that we meet, new ideas enter our world. We buy art that doesn't fit into our collection space, so the question of how to show these pieces comes up— because still it is clear: art should not be locked up in crates, but wants to be exhibited and seen.

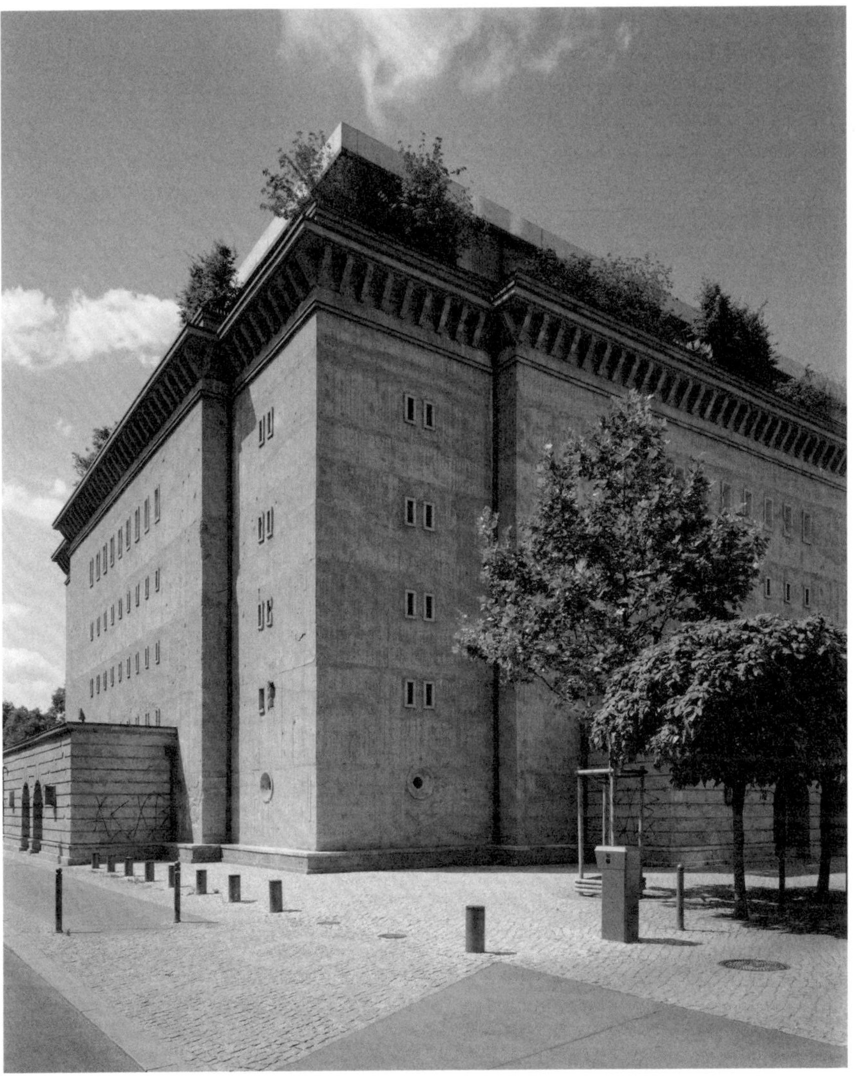

The Bunker, Boros Collection, Berlin

Eli Broad
The Broad Museum, Los Angeles

Eli Broad is the founder of both SunAmerica Inc. and KB Home (formerly Kaufman and Broad Home Corporation). Today, Eli Broad and his wife, Edythe, are devoted to philanthropy as founders of The Broad Foundation, which they established to advance entrepreneurship for the public good in education, science, and the arts.

Year of foundation: 2015
Size: 120,000 square-foot (including the headquarters of The Broad Art Foundation's worldwide lending library of contemporary art)
Employees: 228 employees
Visitors: c. 1.5 million (since opening in 2015)

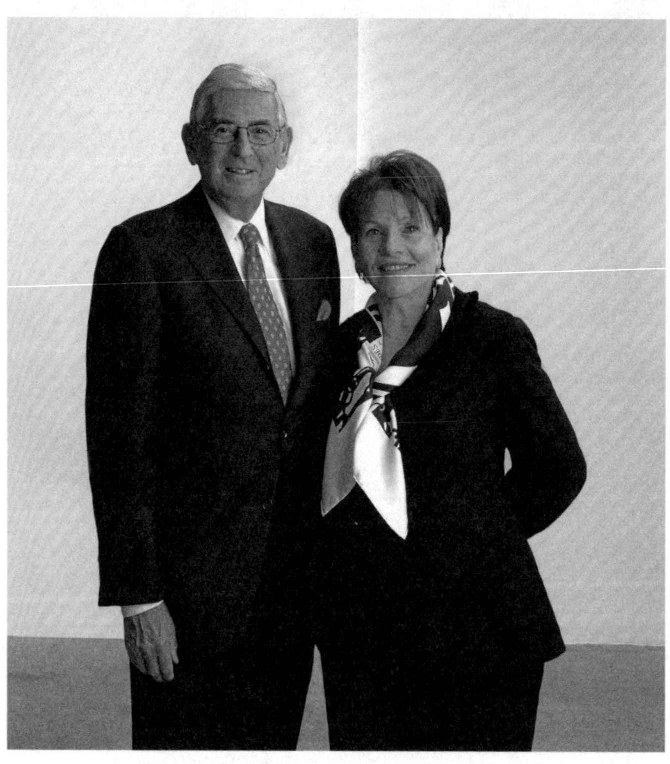

*What was your main motivation in
founding a museum?*

My wife Edythe and I have been
collecting art for decades. In 1984,
we created The Broad Art
Foundation as a lending library
of contemporary art because
we wanted our collection to reach
the widest possible audience.
We initially thought we would
donate our collection to one or
more museums. But after thinking
it over, we realized that by keeping
the collection together and
building a home for it, we could
reach a much wider audience and
make sure it always stayed public.

*Did you have a specific model in mind,
and is there a tradition in your family
of collecting art?*

We drew inspiration from excellent
institutions like The Frick
Collection in New York and the
Norton Simon Museum in
Pasadena, which demonstrated

how appealing a private collection could be to the public. But we had no specific model in mind because we wanted to create a new model for the American museum. We wanted to be as accessible as possible and as welcoming as possible.

What is the focus of your collection? Do you focus on the presentation of your collection or on organizing temporary exhibitions?

The focus of our collection is postwar and contemporary art. We both present our collection and organize exhibitions of loaned works. On the third floor of our museum we show pieces from the collection. On the first floor, we host other exhibitions. Some are drawn from our collection, like the Cindy Sherman exhibition, and others are visiting loan exhibitions. In October 2017 we were one of three American museums to host *Yayoi Kusama: Infinity Mirrors*, and in February 2018 we will become the only US museum to host *Jasper Johns: Something Resembling Truth*.

How did you choose the location of the museum?

When Edythe and I moved to Los Angeles in 1963, the city had no center. Downtown was mostly abandoned. Over time, I became involved with making downtown the heart of Los Angeles again. I was the founding chairman of the Museum of Contemporary Art. Along with Mayor Richard Riordan I raised funds to build the Walt Disney Concert Hall. And I worked with the city and the county to create the Grand Avenue Project, a joint effort to redevelop Grand Avenue.
    I initially considered putting the museum in Santa Monica or Beverly Hills. But downtown was a better choice.

How did you choose the architect?

We held an architectural competition. We ultimately chose Diller Scofidio + Renfro because Elizabeth Diller had a great vision for the museum. She called it "the veil and the vault." The building had to sit across the street from Disney Hall. We didn't want it to compete, but we didn't want it to be anonymous either. Elizabeth had a great idea with the veil wrapping the building and a vault that visitors can look inside to hold our collection.

How involved are you in running the museum?

Edythe and I care a great deal about the museum and its success. We are often in touch with The Broad's founding director, Joanne Heyler, who does an excellent job managing The Broad and its team.

Do you have an educational program?

We are proud that The Broad is really reinventing the American museum. One way we do that is by having a welcoming environment that encourages everyone to learn about art. Instead of uniformed guards, we have visitor services associates who keep the art safe, but also are experts on the works. They interact with visitors and offer insight into the collection. In addition, we host several thousand students every year through a special program. We pay for their transport so schools don't have to rent buses. We invite them here before the museum opens so they get to see everything without crowds, and we help them discuss art and write poetry inspired by the works. We also have free family weekends several times a year.

What is your relationship with public or other institutions?
Do you get public or private funding?

Edythe and I have been supporting arts institutions in Los Angeles and across the country for decades. We have worked hard to help Los Angeles become a cultural capital of the world. We are honored that we have had the ability to build The Broad and open it to the public with free general admission. The Broad is funded by our family. A few of our programs, such as our summer events, are sponsored by others.

In the past five years, what has been your greatest joy in running the museum? And the biggest challenge?

Well, I don't run the museum—our founding director, Joanne Heyler, does that. I think we would agree that the greatest joy is also the greatest challenge. We are delighted that so many people want to visit The Broad.

Lines sometimes wrap all the way around the block. It's great that so many people are interested in contemporary art, but it is also a challenge to make sure we can accommodate everybody.

What can a private museum do, that public institutions cannot? How do you respond to people who criticize the proliferation of private museums?

For a private museum, we are very public. More than 1.5 million people have visited The Broad. We are fortunate to be able to focus on the core work of a museum—sharing art with wide audiences. We don't have to focus on fund-raising, and we have no membership program. We can also act quickly and nimbly because we don't have a large bureaucracy.

What are the greatest challenges in the long-term development of a private museum? What are your plans for the next generation?

Edythe and I built The Broad to live on long past our lifetimes. We are fortunate to be able to endow the museum and ensure that it can continue welcoming audiences in the future.

Do you have unrealized projects?

For now, Edythe and I are focused on continuing to serve a wide, diverse audience at The Broad, and building on two exciting years. We have been successful beyond what we could have hoped. We are especially pleased that our audience is more diverse and younger than the typical museum-going audience. We hope to keep working to bring more people to The Broad.

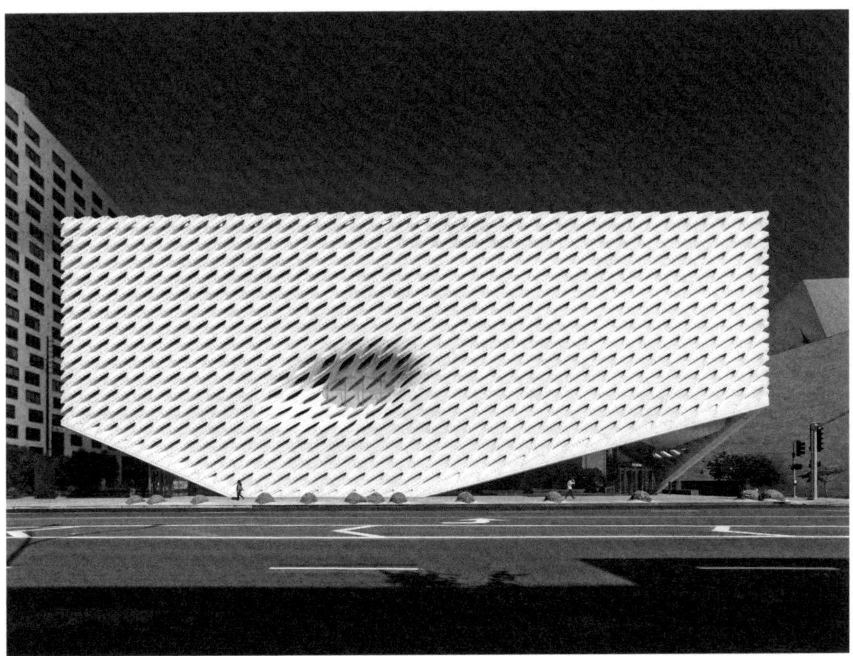

The Broad, Los Angeles

Gil Bronner
Philara Collection, Düsseldorf

Gil Bronner is a real estate developer and art collector. He studied business management in
Cologne. In 2016 Bronner opened his new exhibition space for the Philara collection in Düsseldorf.
The salient feature of the collection is the juxtaposition between local emerging and established
artists.

Year of foundation: 2008 (former space); 2016 (new space)
Size: 2,250 m^2
Number of employees: 17
Visitors: n/a

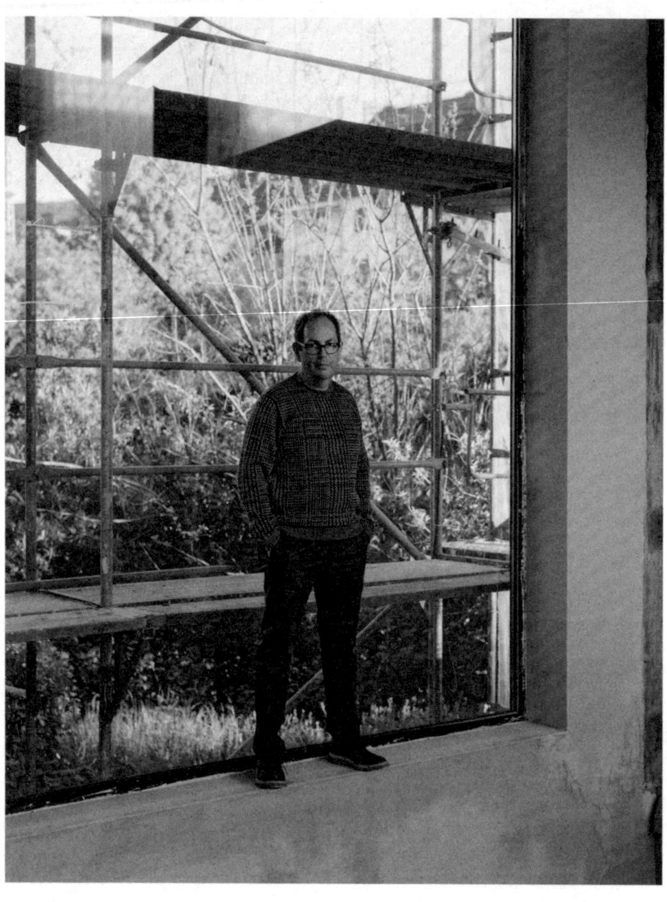

What was your main motivation in founding a museum?

I had actually been showing artists at my old space for quite a while. But the old rooms were relatively far from the city center and difficult to reach. So it was not so much the decision to found a museum that was the motivation to open one, it was more of a logistical consequence of where to house and continuously present a growing collection. It also enables us to show parts of the collection permanently, whereas previously only temporary exhibitions were possible.

Did you have a specific model (i. e. an existing collection) in mind, and is there a tradition in your family of collecting art?

I had no particular model in mind, as I—like probably almost every other collector—like to think the collection is unique. My parents

have been collectors for a long time and I am sure my
children will collect too. So what I am doing is in fact only
a small part of a longer chain.

*What is the focus of your collection? Do you focus on the presentation
of your collection or on organizing temporary exhibitions?*

There is no real focus in the collection. I collect more
or less equally painting, photography, works on paper,
sculptures, and installation works, and, to a lesser degree,
new media. I cannot say that I focus more on one element
in particular. Of course one has the—more or less utopian—
ambition to show as much of the collection as possible.
And I would like to have the opportunity to present younger
artists next to established artists on a more or less permanent basis. By the same token the temporary exhibitions are
an integral part of the Philara's program as it allows the
focus on one or several artists, or on a particular theme.

How did you choose the location of the museum?

A kind of combination of luck and a self-fulfilling prophecy.
In my other life I'm a real estate developer. I bought the
old industrial complex that we now inhabit with business
in mind. As is turned out the area has become the hub
of contemporary galleries in Düsseldorf.

How did you choose the architect?

The architect, Joachim Sieber, is a close friend of mine with
whom I always work. He has had experience building museums before, among others the Galerie der Gegenwart and the
Hubertus-Wald-Forum at the Hamburger Kunsthalle.

*How strongly are you involved in the running of the museum
(programming, management, etc.)?*

I think I am well informed about almost every decision that
is made. I discuss the programming with my director and
generally suggest and contact the artists that we will show.
I try to stay out of decisions regarding personnel planning
and curatorial decisions for actual shows.

Do you have an educational program?

Not yet. But we want to. We have started to contact local schools to see what makes sense.

What is your relationship with public and other institutions?
Do you get (public or private) funding?

We are totally privately funded. We try to generate some funds by renting out the main floor for events, but this only covers a small proportion of the costs.

In the past five years, what has been your greatest joy in running the museum? And what has been the biggest challenge?

It has only been a year. So far I have more or less enjoyed everything. The ongoing challenge is to finally finish all the technical details of the building, and the long-term challenge will be to create a program that is on a sophisticated level without being too intellectual, thereby appealing to all types of visitors. And to continuously take care not to let costs get out of hand.

What can a private museum do, that public institutions cannot?
How do you respond to people who criticize the proliferation of private museums?

Private museums can generally be more spontaneous and react faster than public institutions due to flatter hierarchical structures. The proliferation is a sign of the times. There is nothing to criticize when people use their private money to offer something to the public. Nobody is forced to visit. The argument that museums are used to manipulate markets is also very weak. Who says that private individuals are more easily influenced than people working for public institutions?

What are the greatest challenges in the long-term development of a private museum? What are your plans for the next generation?

As I mentioned before, maintaining a certain standard that is interesting and keeping costs under control. We are so

young we are not planning for the next generation yet.
We have just opened the sculpture terrace; next will be an
accessible storage showroom.

Do you have unrealized projects?

I would like to develop collaborations with other institutions.
Not only with other museums, but also ballet companies,
theaters, concert halls, and such like.

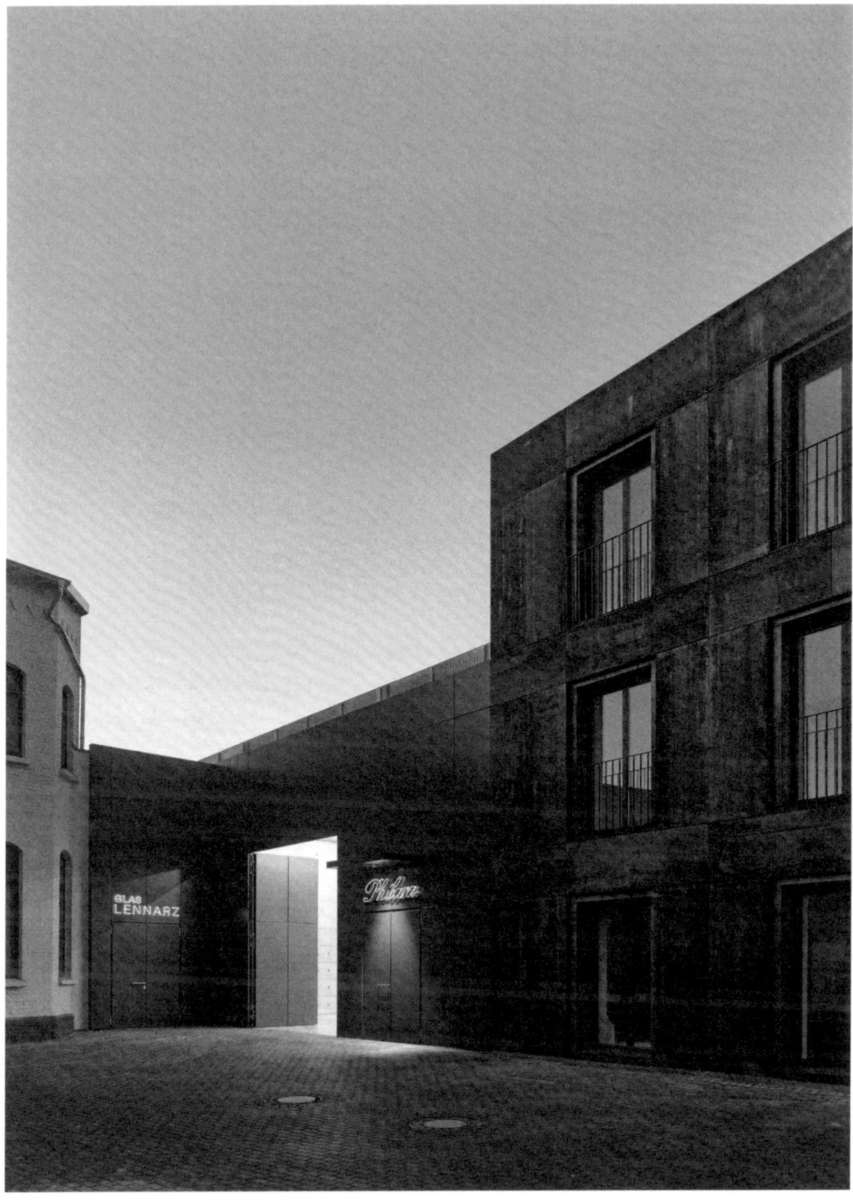

Philara Collection, Düsseldorf

Dimitris Daskalopoulos
NEON, Athens

Dimitris Daskalopoulos is an entrepreneur, the founder and a member of the board of DAMMA Holdings SA, a financial services and investment participations company. He is a collector of contemporary art and the founder of NEON, a nonprofit organization that aims to bring contemporary culture closer to everyone.

Year of foundation: 2013
Size: nomadic
Number of employees: n/a
Visitors: n/a

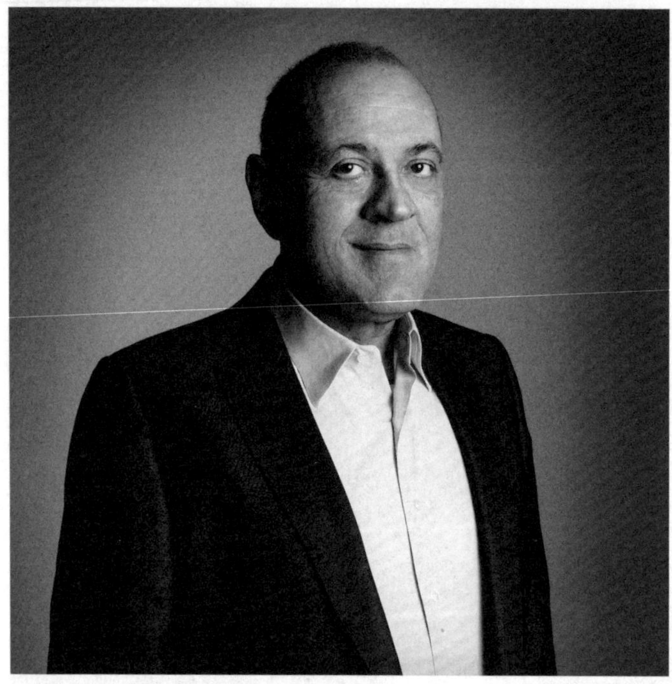

Your foundation NEON isn't a private art museum, but operates in different places and contexts. What ideas is NEON based on, and how exactly does it work?

NEON is an itinerant, nomadic undertaking that seeks to expose the widest public to the ideas and challenges of contemporary creativity in art, which can stimulate, inspire, and affect the individual and society at large. It has two founding and governing principles: a) it does not have its own museum, building, or space and b) it is not about showing or promoting the Dimitris Daskalopoulos Collection. In that sense, we have been able to remain free and extrovert, to focus not on ourselves, but on the visitors that we want to attract, to reach different audiences in many areas of the cities in Greece, to give the opportunity to curators and artists to create innovative events and artworks. We are free to imagine from a bird's eye view instead of

looking at or shouting at the world from the confines of
our room.

Did you have a specific model in mind?

I usually try to learn from models by breaking them. I was
aware of the pitfalls and constraints of the various models
already employed by private collectors and tried to avoid
them. That is why I am experimenting with my own.

*What is your relationship with institutions and spaces you are
involved with? Do you get other (public or private) funding?*

NEON constructively collaborates with cultural institutions
and supports the programs of public and private institutions
to enhance increased access and inventive interaction with
contemporary art. We seek to locate, reveal, and animate
existing public and private spaces. We aim to generate
maximum attractiveness for the public to visit. We choose
spaces that give artists a strong stimulus to create new
and different works. Our funding is 100% private (my own)
and all our events are free to the public.

*How strongly are you involved in the running of NEON
(programming, management, etc.)?*

I am privileged to benefit from the contribution and passion
of a dedicated group of able people who require only my
vision and general guidance.

What is the focus of your educational program?

The Greek school curriculum does not reflect the artistic
inspirations, talent, trends, and needs of local communities
in the field of the visual arts.
     Our program "Is this Art?" is focused on reaching out
annually to thousands of teens in public and private schools
through a tailor-made youth-interactive platform that is both
online and physically engaging. We build on the freedom
of choice and opportunities that the reality of a non-space
gives us. We work with the educators, local communities,
and in alignment with the needs and aspirations of society.

For our public outreach we focus on initiatives that promote learning and inspiration in communities across ages and social groups. It is rewarding to nourish and shape the vibrancy and diversity of the local cultural ecology.

In the past four years, what has been your greatest joy in running the project? What has been the biggest challenge?

My greatest joy comes when I see a family huddled around an artwork discussing it, or when a young child points at an artwork and asks a question, or when someone in an exhibition sits on the floor and closes their eyes. I am happy to see that our initiatives are touching people.

Challenges? The only challenges in any creative process are to keep up with your dreams and to avoid repeating past mistakes.

What is the focus of your own art collection and why did you decide not to create a museum for your collection?

The collection is imbued with the principle that collecting is about creating a rich web of relationships among artworks, whose connected totality of meaning is more complex than the simple sum of all single artworks in the collection. It is interesting to note that the etymological root of the Greek word collect (συλλέγω) means "saying something with."

The collection's inner compass is a magnetic orientation toward the most elemental, diachronic, and age-old issue of the human condition. Among the themes that run through the collection, the notion of the body as a source of creativity and the vessel of existential, social, and ideological struggle is a compelling and repeatedly examined motif.

I did not build a museum because I believe that an art collection is driven by the passion of an individual and expresses their mentality. When the driver is gone, the collection becomes a capsule in time. I find that a private museum is more about "HIM" than about art. Over time, it becomes about "THEN" and not about contemporary art. Over even more time, any collection in any private museum becomes irrelevant because it cannot keep abreast of and in dialogue with contemporary creativity.

How do you work with your collection? Is it shown in other museums?

The Dimitris Daskalopoulos Collection considers its role to be that of a temporary custodian of the physical manifestation of great ideas and artistic creativity.

The collection's physical objects are treated as a repository to be utilized by institutions and curators, and as an open resource to interact with other private or public collections or institutions toward disseminating art's essential message.

It is in this spirit that the collection has had a long-standing open lending policy, and has made its holdings available to public institutions that choose to present curated exhibitions drawing on the Dimitris Daskalopoulos Collection to their audiences.

Do you have unrealized projects?

So many that I need to live at least four more lives!

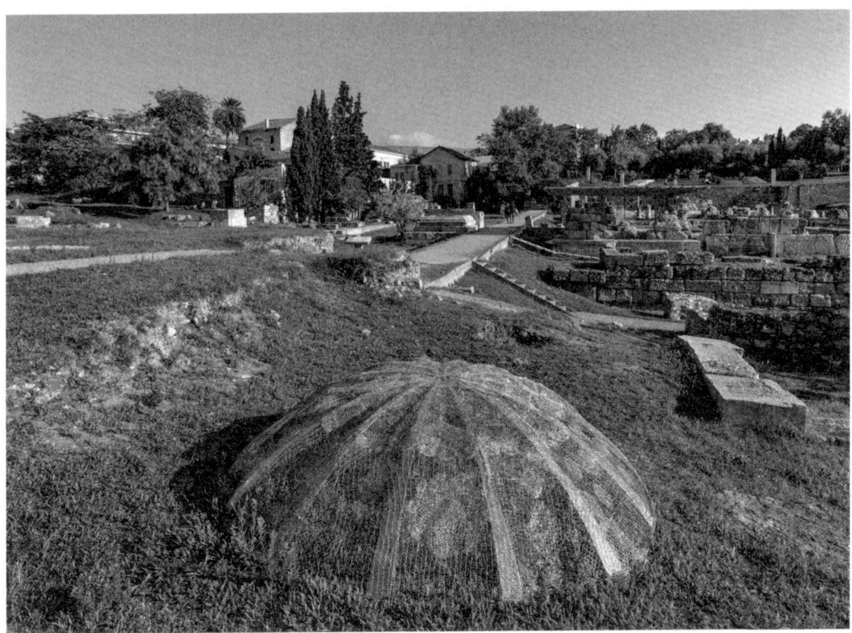

Maria Loizidou, *A Transfer*, Kerameikos Museum and Archaeological Site, City Project Commission
2015 by NEON, 2015

Jens Faurschou
Faurschou Foundation, Copenhagen and Beijing

Jens Faurschou is an art collector and art adviser. In 1986 he established the Galleri Faurschou in Copenhagen together with his then-wife Luise. After closing the gallery they founded the Faurschou Foundation in 2011, which is based in Copenhagen and Beijing.

Year of foundation: 2011
Size (w/o office areas): 900 m^2 (Copenhagen); 400 m^2 (Beijing)
Number of employees: 13 (Copenhagen), 4 (Beijing)
Visitors: 60,000–70,000 a year (Beijing), around 6,000 a year (Copenhagen)

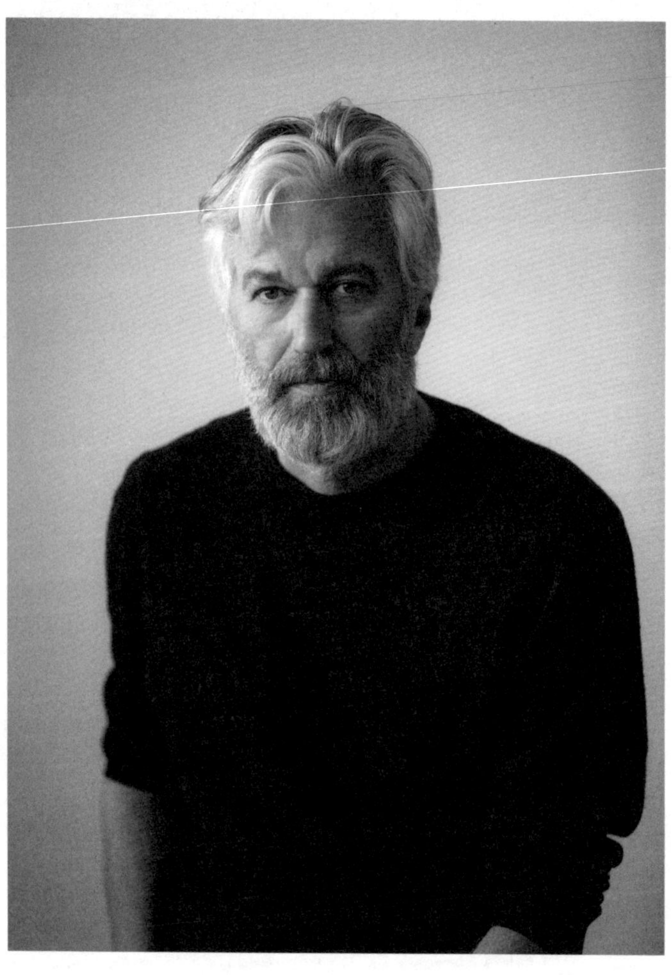

What was your main motivation in founding a museum?

Today the Faurschou Foundation is located in two exhibition spaces, but it's not a museum per se. I started as a gallerist, and over the last 20 years I have been building a vast art collection in the process. At one point I realized that my drive is to make great exhibitions, and my ambition is to show artworks of greater scale to larger audiences. So when the right opportunity presented itself we opened exhibition spaces in beautiful locations in China and Denmark.

Did you have a specific model (i.e. an existing collection) in mind, and is there a tradition in your family of collecting art?

My family has no history with art. I was a pioneer in that respect and was creating and following my dreams along the way.

What is the focus of your collection? Do you focus on the presentation of your collection or on organizing temporary exhibitions?

The collection consists of several hundred pieces, so we can only show them selectively whenever they fit in the context of the exhibition. Our focus is on organizing meaningful and historically relevant exhibitions, and we often choose to combine works from our collection with those borrowed from elsewhere to best support the subject of a given theme.

How did you choose the location of the museum?

By chance I got to visit the 798 Art District in Beijing in 2006. There was so much going on there, however not many galleries in China were showing the major Western artists at the time. There was a gap to be filled and I felt that we could make a difference. On the same trip we were offered a great space at 798, and I fell in love with it.

How did you choose the architect?

We did not build the buildings of the two exhibition spaces, rather just partially transformed their interior. In Copenhagen we worked with architect Jakob Møller. We also have our own in-house architect, Kristian Eley, who is in charge of designing the architecture for each new exhibition.

How strongly are you involved in the running of the museum (programming, management, etc.)?

I am closely involved in planning the program of the exhibition spaces, making new acquisitions, and taking other crucial decisions, driven by my vision. My team deals with the implementation of ideas down to the smallest details.

Do you have an educational program?

We do not have a dedicated educational program, but we encourage local schools to bring their pupils to visit the exhibitions at our spaces and to learn more about contemporary art.

*What is your relationship with public or other institutions? Do you get
(public or private) funding?*

We do not get external funding, but we sometimes collabo-
rate with other institutions for specific exhibitions. For
example, we collaborated with Fondazione Giorgio Cini in
Venice to show an exhibition in their space in 2015 and again
in the summer of 2017 for a series of three exhibitions—
*Robert Rauschenberg & Andy Warhol: Us Silkscreeners … ; Robert
Rauschenberg: Late Series*; *Paul McCarthy and Christian Lemmerz:
New Media Art (Virtual Reality Art).*

*In the past five years, what has been your greatest joy in running
the museum? What has been the biggest challenge?*

There are many joys; something I particularly like is
witnessing the transformation of our spaces in-between
the exhibitions, especially in Copenhagen, where we have
managed each time to reshape the architecture to maximize
the impression of the exhibited art. When you come to
a new exhibition you get a feeling of visiting a completely
different space. We never compromise, always going all
the way. The greatest challenge is to keep on funding the
ambitious exhibition program, but somehow we always
succeed.

What can a private museum do, that public institutions cannot?

We can break the budget again and again, which is impossible
for a public institution.

*How do you respond to people who criticize the proliferation
of private museums?*

I have never met such people.

*What are the greatest challenges in the long-term development
of a private museum?*

To keep up with being relevant to society.

What are your plans for the next generation?

To train their eye.

Do you have unrealized projects?

Many of my projects actually come to life and I am sure
I will keep coming up with new ideas. Faurschou Foundation
is expanding, opening new spaces in New York and in the
Napa Valley, so there are a lot of sublime exhibition ideas yet
to be realized.

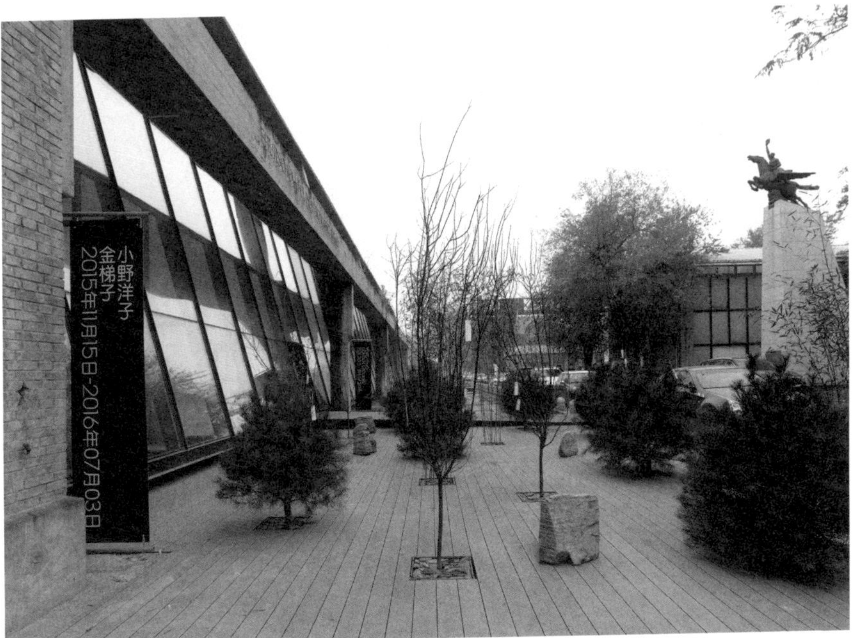

View of the exhibition *Yoko Ono: Golden Ladders*, Faurschou Foundation, Beijing, 2015

Soichiro Fukutake
Benesse Art Site Naoshima, Seto Inland Sea

Soichiro Fukutake is honorary adviser and former chairman of Benesse Holdings Inc., a Japanese company providing a wide range of educational services, senior care, and language courses. Presiding over Benesse Art Site Naoshima since its inception, Fukutake has spearheaded the Seto Inland Sea renaissance around the Naoshima, Teshima, and Inujima islands, focused on art, nature, and architecture for the past 30 years.

Year of foundation: 1987
Size: three islands Naoshima, Teshima, and Inujima (includes eight art museums and multiple art facilities)
Number of employees: 304 (as of 2016)
Visitors: 608,642 museum entries (April 2015–March 2016)

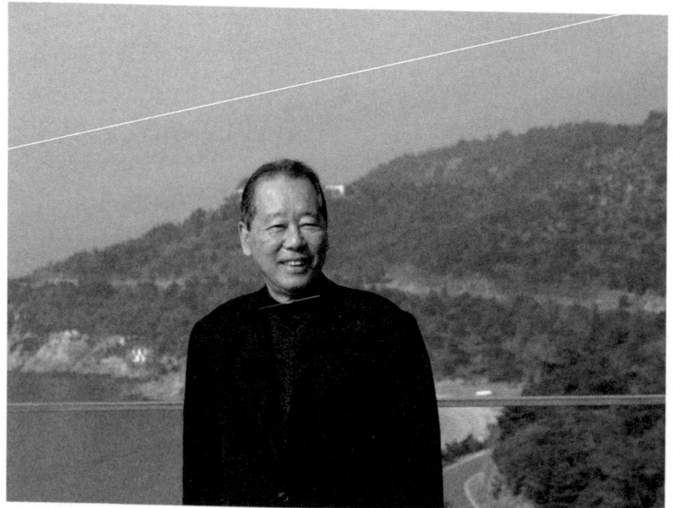

What was your main motivation in founding a museum?

The original impetus leading to the creation of Benesse Art Site Naoshima was a desire to participate in the development of Naoshima. One of my father's dreams was to create a campsite for children on the island. As he passed away while the project was still evolving, I decided to honor his will and created the campsite. Thirty years later, the project has developed into an art site encompassing three islands in the Seto Inland Sea: Naoshima, Teshima, and Inujima.

Visiting the area to oversee the project I came to realize how Naoshima's natural environment had been damaged by the toxic emanations from the copper refinery built on the island—even though the Setouchi region had been designated the first national park of Japan. On the neighboring island Teshima also, huge quantities of industrial waste had been dumped illegally. This triggered a deep sense of anger against the excesses of modernization and urbanization that led to such dire consequences, and a strong desire to use contemporary art as a weapon to enact resistance to this state of modern society. These feelings have only grown stronger with time.

Our approach to using art as a medium to revitalize the dwindling population of the islands and bring renewed energy to the local community and its predominantly elderly population—thus creating an environment envied by visitors from metropolitan areas—is now being referred to as the "Naoshima Method," and is increasingly gathering attention as an effective method to reduce the divide between rural and urban areas.

Did you have a specific model (i.e. an existing collection) in mind, and is there a tradition in your family of collecting art?

I cannot think of any example of an art museum built on an island ravaged by excessive industrialization, so no, there was no direct reference. But the Louisiana Museum of Modern Art in Humlabæk with its maritime backdrop left a lasting impression on me.

What is the focus of your collection? Do you focus on the presentation of your collection or on organizing temporary exhibitions?

As mentioned, my interest lies in resisting excessive modernization and industrialization, so the works I acquire tend to express this line of thought. Another clear focus is to create permanent exhibition spaces.

In order to maximize the message emanating from each artwork, both the natural and architectural environments in which they are presented play a crucial role. I thus strive to work alongside the motto "one artist, one gallery," dedicating a single exhibition space to each artist in most of the galleries spread over the islands.

Furthermore, our work at Benesse Art Site Naoshima doesn't consist in exhibiting artworks in the sterile, white-cube architecture that defines most museums. Rather, by inserting art into the natural context of the islands, we create an environment where it is possible to reflect on the conditions and meaning of well-being, and offer a range of experiences that cannot possibly be replicated in an urban context. This is why our activities are mainly concentrated on the three islands of Naoshima, Inujima, and Teshima.

How did you choose the location of the museum?

I personally select the optimal location for each museum, on foot, by car, by boat, or by piloting my helicopter around potential sites.

How did you choose the architect?

Since my initial aim was to resist against modern society, and with Tokyo embodying all the ills of our age, I decided from the beginning to exclude any architect living in that city. I chose to work with Tadao Ando, since he lived in Osaka, and because of his fighting spirit—Ando used to be a professional boxer. Our collaboration has extended over the past 30 years. In recent years, Kazuyo Sejima and Ryue Nishizawa from SANAA, as well as Hiroshi Sambuichi have also participated in our activities.

How strongly are you involved in the running of the museum (programming, management, etc.)?

Being the Chairman of the Fukutake Foundation, I personally make the decisions in terms of the selection of artists, and I also define our strategic matrix—in consultation with my staff.

Do you have an educational program?

We offer programs for children, and also have a focus on visual thinking strategies to encourage discussion-based, experience-based art viewing.

What is your relationship with public or other institutions? Do you get (public or private) funding?

We have developed close working ties with the local authorities on all three islands over the years, but do not receive any public funding for our activities.

The main operating body, Fukutake Foundation, covers its expenses from the dividends paid out by Benesse Holdings Inc. (the Foundation owns 5% of the Benesse stock), from donations by the Fukutake family, and from the income generated by museum admissions and shop sales. In future, I believe it will be increasingly important that entities responsible for the operation of privately funded arts or cultural initiatives directly own shares of the profit-making company backing them. We call this model "Public Interest Capitalism" and I am very keen to advocate this approach globally.

In the past five years, what has been your greatest joy in running the museum? What has been the biggest challenge?

When we started our activities on Naoshima, at first it was difficult for local people to accept us because what we were doing was so different from the island's traditions. It was thus a great source of joy to be named an honorary citizen of Naoshima a few years into our project.

We completed the Chichu Art Museum in 2004, and I was again really happy when I acquired the fifth and last painting of Monet's *Water Lilies* series, which was permanently installed in the museum in 2009, after an extensive and very arduous search around the world. I was also really thrilled when the first edition of the Setouchi Triennale—of which I am the General Producer—successfully launched on seven islands in the Seto Inland Sea in 2010. There are many other examples.

The reason for so many joyful milestones is that the activities of Benesse Art Site Naoshima are clearly geared at creating a happy environment for the local community and its people. Art is not the end purpose in itself, rather I believe that art has the power to revitalize local, peripheral regions left behind in our modern age.

What can a private museum do, that public institutions cannot? How do you respond to people who criticize the proliferation of private museums?

I find it hard to believe that there may be criticism directed at the increasing number of private museums. My feeling is that many public museums lack individuality. This is probably because it is difficult to create an institution with a strong character when the decision-making is democratically shared among a large number of actors.

My belief is that a model where companies—which are the sole source of economic wealth creation in society—establish foundations, systematically entrust part of their shares to the foundations (rather than making sporadic donations to cultural causes), and where these foundation take the lead to contribute to the cultural development of the regions in which each company is rooted, such a model will be mutually beneficial to both the companies and the development of culture itself. To those claiming that economic development should be our central concern, I respond that economy is a servant to culture.

What are the greatest challenges in the long-term development of a private museum? And what are your plans for the next generation?

There have not been any insurmountable challenges to date. As approximately 40% of the project's income is covered by dividend revenue from Benesse Holdings, smooth management of the company is of course essential. But we are also creating a model to ensure that the art initiative can be operated even in the eventuality that the dividend stream dried up. In terms of the next generation, I strongly hope that my successor will remain faithful to the core philosophy developed at Benesse Art Site Naoshima.

Do you have unrealized projects?

I still have many ideas.

My dream was to create an earthly paradise through the medium of art. Most religions postulate that true happiness will be bestowed upon us after death. This may be true, but I still think that heaven should be found in the here and now.

Everyone wants to lead a happy life, but that is of course not easy to achieve. I believe that to become truly happy, one needs to live in a happy community. What defines a happy community? I got to understand that a happy community is a place filled with the smiles of seniors—

who are masters of life. On the islands of the Seto Inland
Sea, one does not find many things—information or
entertainment. Such material commodities will in fact not
lead to a joyful life. On the other hand, the islands are
blessed with a wonderful natural environment and with the
presence of the elderly and their lifelong experiences.

Nowadays, many young people have come to live on
these islands, and the elderly also have become very vibrant.
The path I have walked, one of using art—of employing
the "Naoshima Method"—for the past 30 years has taught
me that indeed it *is* possible to experience heaven on earth.

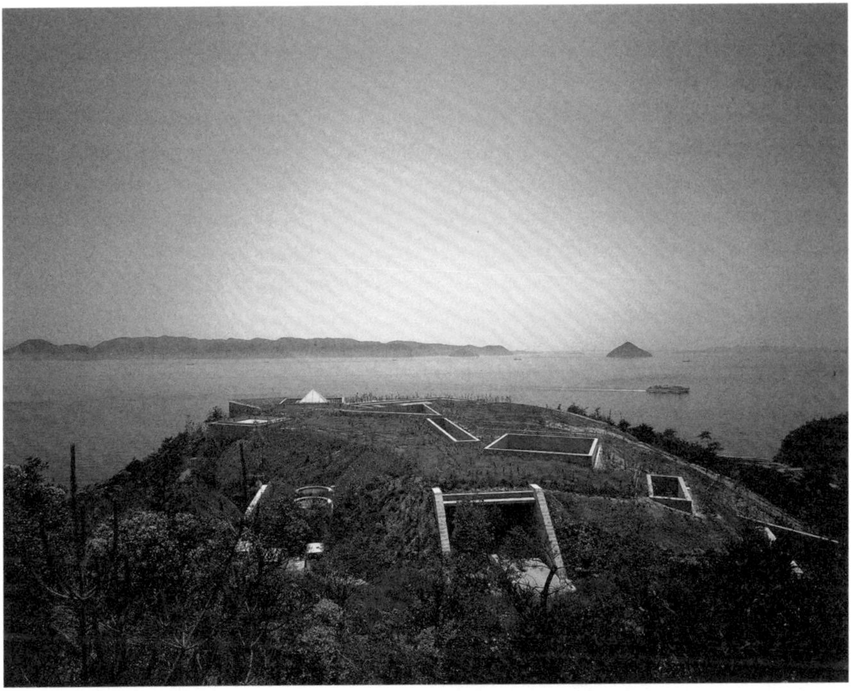

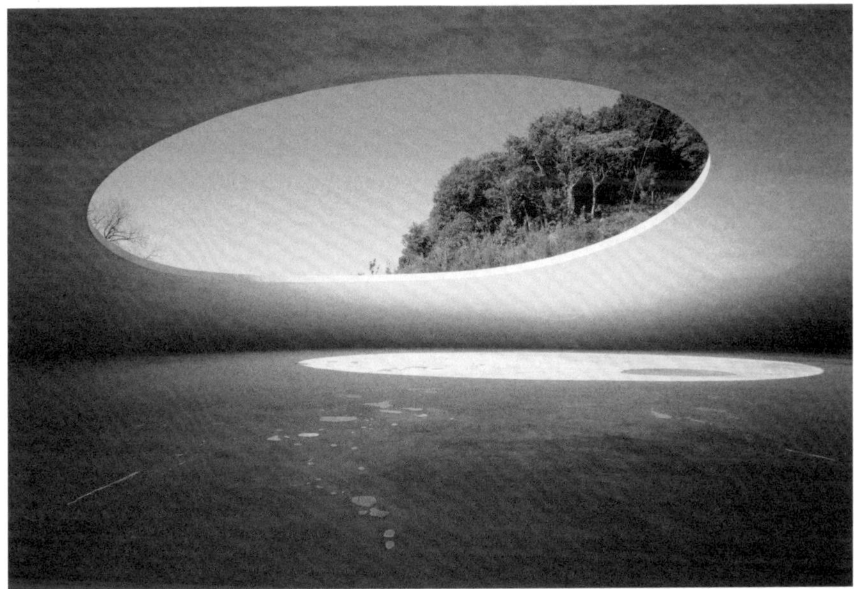

Chichu Art Museum, Benesse Art Site Naoshima, Naoshima
Teshima Art Museum, Benesse Art Site Naoshima, Teshima

Ingvild Goetz
Goetz Collection, Munich

Ingvild Goetz founded a publishing studio in Konstanz in 1969. In 1972, she opened the gallery Art in Progress in Zurich, relocating it to Munich in 1973. Since the gallery's closure in 1984, she has devoted her time to the systematic expansion of her collection, which focuses on Arte Povera, American artists of the 1980s, Young British Artists, and the individual positions of German artists.

Year of foundation: 1990 (the building was completed in 1993)
Size: c. 700 m^2
Number of employees: 15
Visitors: n/a

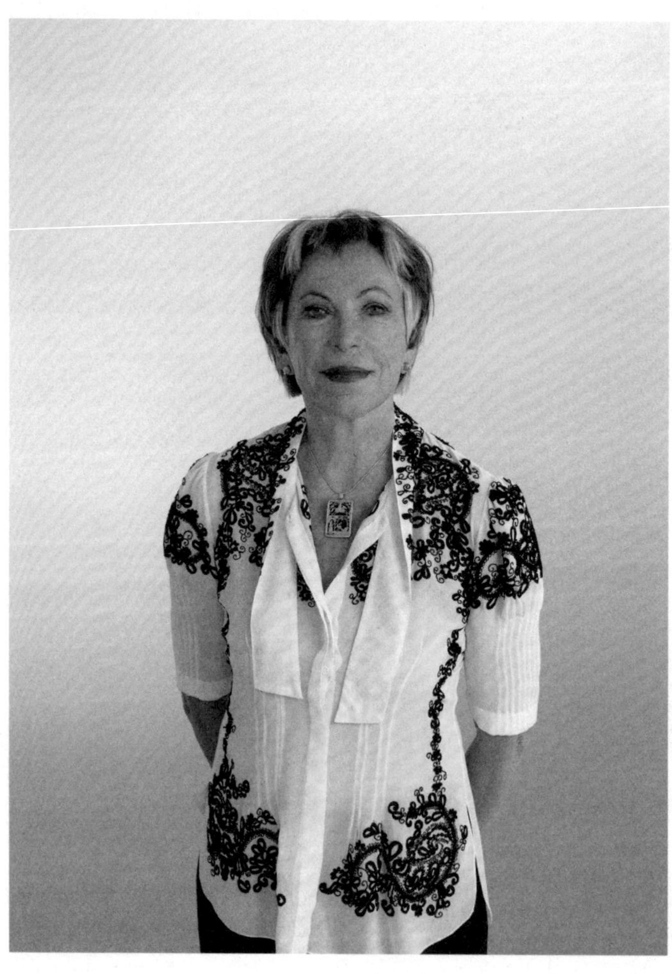

What was your main motivation in founding a museum?

I wanted to take my extensive collection out of the depot and look at it in different exhibitions. In my own museum I have access to it all the time, and I can sit in front of my works for as long as I like. Besides, I enjoy curating, and I can combine the works according to my own ideas, and thus see them in various contexts.

Did you have a specific model (i.e. an existing collection) in mind, and is there a tradition of collecting art in your family?

No, I didn't have any model because at the time I founded my museum there were no private museums in Germany, apart from the Museum Insel Hombroich. And I didn't know of any in the rest of Europe either. We had important artworks at home, but there were no collectors in my family.

What is the focus of your collection? Do you focus on the presentation of your collection or on organizing temporary exhibitions?

During my time as a gallerist I only collected sporadically. The building up of the collection began when I closed the gallery in the mid-1980s, and has been concentrated since then on Arte Povera, the art of the respective present, and works by selected artists. I take the entire spectrum of today's artistic forms of expression into account. As well as drawings, prints, paintings, sculptures, photographs, and spatial installations there is a focus on video, film, and multi-projections. We largely curate our exhibitions from the collection's holdings—more than 5,000 works at present. It's an inexhaustible resource, from which constantly new thematic aspects can be developed for interesting exhibitions.

How did you choose the location of the museum?

I wanted a museum in direct proximity to my home, so as to give me the possibility of looking often and intensively at my works of art.

How did you choose the architect?

I looked around a lot, and asked architects if they could realize my idea of a private museum. But it was unsatisfactory. Artist Helmut Federle and gallerist Rosemarie Schwarzwälder then introduced us to Jacques Herzog and Pierre de Meuron, two then still unknown young architects. Even the first cursory sketch convinced me of the rightness of their concept. Thankfully they still had a lot of time in those days, and were able to oversee the construction.

How strongly are you involved in the running of the museum (programming, management, etc.)?

Until the donation of my museum and part of my collection to the Free State of Bavaria on January 1, 2014, I was involved in all areas. Since then I have withdrawn somewhat, and leave most of it to my very good staff. But I maintain an overview and continue to extend the collection through new acquisitions.

Do you have an educational program?

We offer an extensive side program for all the exhibitions, with artists' talks, readings, podium discussions, and guided tours. And there are also special workshops with art educators for children and unaccompanied refugees.

What is your relationship with public or other institutions? Do you get (public or private) funding?

We show works in our collection in various exhibition projects with cooperating partners around the world, and we support other institutions with loans. Until the donation in 2014 I financed everything myself and received no support of any kind. Since then the Bavarian state covers the running costs and I only pay for special projects.

In the past five years, what has been your greatest joy in running the museum? What has been the biggest challenge?

For me the greatest challenge has been the different exhibitions we have curated from our collection for other museums, for example the Fundación Banco Santander in Madrid, the Museion in Bozen, the Kunsthalle München, the Pinakothek der Moderne, the Museum Villa Stuck, and the Haus der Kunst (all in Munich). With the Haus der Kunst we have built a lasting partnerhip to show video art from the Goetz Collection permanently.

The greatest joy has been the recognition of my work through awards, such as the Bavarian Order of Merit, the prize from the Konrad Adenauer Foundation, the Montblanc de la Culture Arts Patronage Award, the Art Cologne Prize, the Order of Merit of the Federal Republic, and so on.

What can a private museum do, that public institutions cannot? How do you respond to people who criticize the proliferation of private museums?

As a private person you can take swift purchasing decisions, because there isn't a committee. You can also try daring exhibitions, as a private museum doesn't have as much responsibility to the public as a state institution financed

by taxes. For me it was important to enter into a partnership
with public museums, as private collections can close gaps
through loans or donations, because the acquisition budget
for these institutions is now practically non-existent.
But I think it is equally legitimate for a private collector
to do the museum work alone and allow the public to share
in it.

*What are the greatest challenges in the long-term development of
a private museum? What are your plans for the next generation?*

A private museum can experiment, free from all influences,
with different exhibition formats; it can take on risky
projects, show young artists early on, and thus act quite
differently from the public museums. The next generation
will realize its own plans.

Do you have any unrealized projects?

I still have a lot of interesting ideas for new exhibition
projects, and look forward to realizing them in the future.

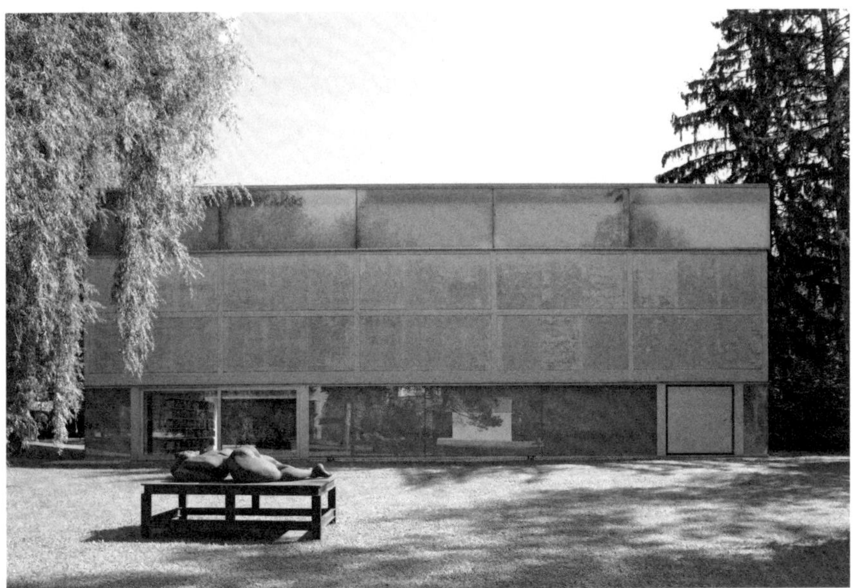

Goetz Collection, Munich

Dakis Joannou
Deste Foundation for Contemporary Art, Athens

Dakis Joannou is an industrialist and art collector. He studied engineering and architecture.
He is the president of the Deste Foundation for Contemporary Art, which was established in 1983.
In addition to the Deste Foundation in Athens he initiated the Deste Prize and a Project Space
located on the Greek island Hydra.

Year of foundation: 1983
Size: c. 2,000 m^2 (Athens); c. 30 m^2 (Hydra)
Number of employees: 5
Visitors: n/a

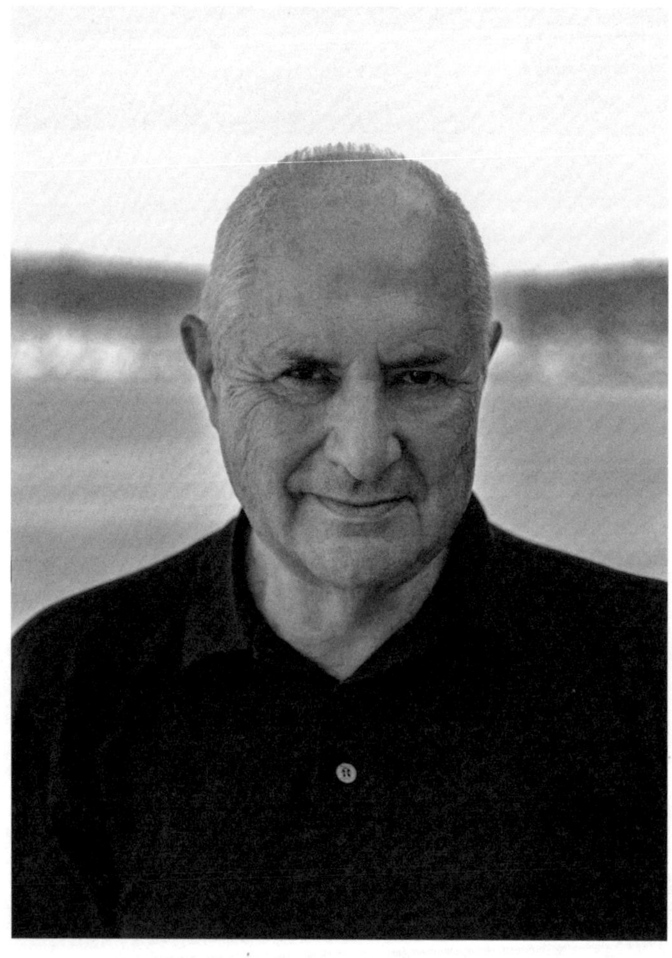

*What was your main motivation in
founding a museum?*

Deste is not a museum; it's a
foundation that started as a concept.
It was about participating in
the dialogue about art, generating
energy by engaging people, and
creating a platform for pursuing
new ideas.

*Did you have a specific model
(i.e. an existing collection) in mind,
and is there a tradition in your family
of collecting art?*

We invented our own model.
We have no program, but quickly
respond to new ideas and develop
a project only when it excites us.

*What is the focus of your collection?
Do you focus on the presentation of your
collection or on organizing temporary
exhibitions?*

The focus of the collection is contemporary art, in fact art after 1985.

We only organize temporary exhibitions and they are based
on the collection to the extent that they fit the concept.

How did you choose the location of the museum?

We have moved to a few spaces, now we are hosted regularly
by a couple of Greek museums, the Benaki Museum and the
Museum of Cycladic Art, and occasionally by European
museums. In addition we operate the Hydra Slaughterhouse
every summer and use part of our Athens' Nea Ionia space.

How did you choose the architect?

It's an industrial building and we do all work in-house.

*How strongly are you involved in the running of the museum
(programming, management, etc.)?*

Totally involved.

Do you have an educational program?

No, we are not a museum. The museums that host us run
education programs.

What is your relationship with public or other institutions?
Do you get (public or private) funding?

We are self funded and have excellent relationships
with other institutions.

*In the past five years, what has been your greatest joy in running
the museum? And what has been the biggest challenge?*

The greatest joy is the relationship with artists and other
art people, finding new ideas, and organizing unexpected
and challenging projects.

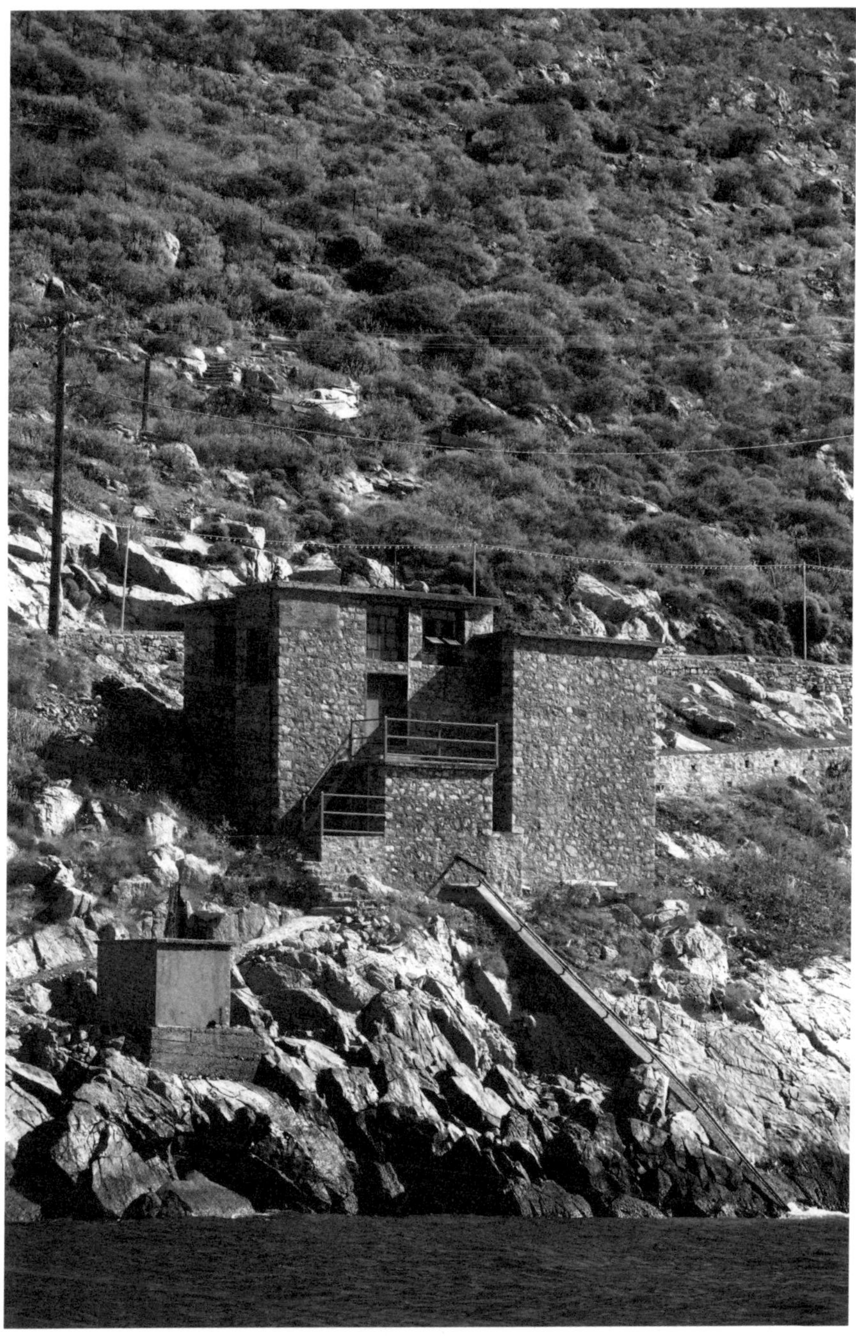

Deste Foundation for Contemporary Art Project Space, Slaughterhouse, Hydra

What can a private museum do, that public institutions cannot?
How do you respond to people who criticize the proliferation of
private museums?

A private institution is free to make quick decisions, stay
relevant and ... make mistakes! I agree with those criticizing
the proliferation of private museums.

What are the greatest challenges in the long-term development of
a private museum? And what are your plans for the next generation?

Tomorrow is another day ...

Do you have any unrealized projects?

Yes.

Grażyna Kulczyk
Muzeum Susch, Zernez

Grażyna Kulczyk is an entrepreneur and art collector. She initiated the Stary Browar culture, business, and shopping complex in a former brewery in Poznań, Poland, in 2003, and the Muzeum Susch in Switzerland.

Year of foundation: 2018
Size: c. 1,200 m^2
Number of employees: c. 10
Visitors: n/a

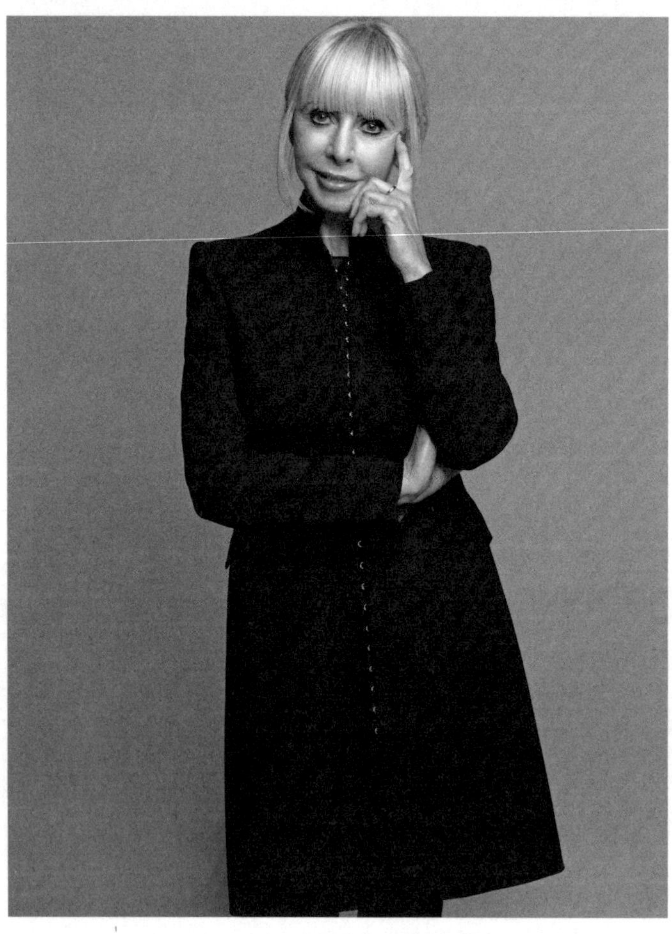

What was your main motivation in founding a museum?

I have been engaged in creating art institutions for many years. In 2004, I finally decided to formalize my art activities, and I initiated the Art Stations Foundation in my hometown, Poznań. This interdisciplinary, Kunsthalle-like institution focused on art and choreography. It was situated in the large Stary Browar complex that is a former industrial site I restored and transformed into a commercial and cultural venue. It was an extremely important project for me, as it created an inspirational urban hub for the city and for the region. It has not only changed the industrial site, but also the debate around social and urban changes in the city. I believe this was achieved by my 50/50 philosophy, that I implemented daily—to dedicate one half for commercial use and the other half for cultural programs. I did not want to be an entrepreneur during

a day and an art aficionado in the evening. This balanced
policy helped me to create a natural and sustainable system.
I now want to dedicate a project to the culturally rich
environment of the Engadin valley, which will rejuvenate
the small, medieval, rural, monastic settlement in the village
of Susch. I'm very fascinated by the sculptural landscape
and the harsh history of this region. Muzeum Susch will
contribute as a cultural institution by creating a place for
debate and the production of contemporary art. This cultural
mission derives from my key concerns and interests:
to engage with radical female artists and to show postwar
Eastern European artists in a global dialogue. I also agree
with the speculations of some specialists that the future
of the museum is downsizing. This gives another perspective
to venues similar to Muzeum Susch.

*Did you have a specific model (i.e. an existing collection) in mind,
and is there a tradition in your family of collecting art?*

The overall model of my collection follows the concept of
the redefinition of the canonical and the marginalized.
Basically I try to reread and question established narratives
in art history. Therefore, at the beginning the collection
really began to support contemporary Polish and Central
Eastern European art, which have long been widely ignored
by Western critics and collectors due to the particular
political environment of former Eastern Bloc states. Beyond
this general ambition, however, my collecting strategy also
reflects other key interests. Since Western artists have been
joining the collection, opening up new perspectives,
and highlighting contrasts between works, as well as raising
questions about the multifarious and complex relations
between East and West in general, have become central
issues.
 These expanded perspectives and contrasts within
the collection provide the basis for commentary on complex
20th- and 21st-century global concerns.
 It is so difficult to refer to collecting family traditions
in Poland when for the past 400 years it has been a European
battlefield. My grandparents' and parents' generation had
to fight for the country's independence (my father was
a military pilot during World War II at the Polish division

within the RAF and returned home ten years to the day after the war had started), and then had to build a fragile stability in postwar Poland step by step. Therefore, I was the first one in family to start collecting. I began when I was a student.

What is the focus of your collection? Do you focus on the presentation of your collection or on organizing temporary exhibitions?

At Muzeum Susch my collection will serve as a pool of ideas. The museum is definitely not a collection depot. I would prefer it to be perceived as an experimental institute. The temporary exhibitions will use the collection as a trigger for thoughts and concepts. Another element in the strategy are several commissions I'm realizing with artists. These works are site-specific and interact directly with the architecture. A beautiful example is a large sculpture by Monika Sosnowska located in the former brewery's ice-tower; it connects the different floors of the building.

How did you choose the location of the museum?

The Engadin has always attracted visitors from far and wide. Leading artists and intellectuals were drawn to the valley and its majestic tranquility. Rainer Maria Rilke, Friedrich Nietzsche, Giovanni Segantini, Ernst Ludwig Kirchner, and many of their counterparts today are similarly inspired by the cinematographic magic of the Engadin. The ancient, regional language Romansh is also a heritage the museum will cultivate.

How did you choose the architect?

I heard about Lukas Voellmy and Chasper Schmidlin from our friends, the gallerists von Bartha. Just after they graduated from ETH these young architects transformed a former garage in Basel into a gallery, and this project attracted my attention. For me it is very important to work with talented Swiss people instead of bringing in an international starchitect. Working with young people often brings unexpected and unusual ideas, which frequently compensate for the potential lack of many years of experience.

*How strongly are you involved in the running of the museum
(programming, management, etc.)?*

The museum is the realization of my vision so I want to be
very involved. But at the same time I have a lot of trust
in my team and friends that support me. Alison Gingeras is
very experienced in feminist art as well as in the management
of the museum as artistic director. Fredi Fischli and Niels
Olsen shared a close dialogue with contemporary artists and
embed the museum in a local context as curators of the
museum's residency program. Eveline Fasser Testa lives in
the Engadin and is managing day-to-day operations on site.
A museum is being defined through our dialogue and
numerous discussions; however in the end it's my vision
and my responsibility for better or for worse.

Do you have an educational program?

Being situated in the Engadin we're not an anonymous
museum in an urban environment; we want to be very close
to anybody who visits us. My goal is to shift the idea of
an educational program to a more interactive program.
This means that we are planning workshops, conferences,
moments when people actually get together and discuss,
not only the exhibitions, but also more general topics like
feminist art, the dialogues between Eastern and Western art,
or any other current concerns, in the same way that the
Engadin Art Talks [Cristina Bechtler has been organizing the
Engadin Art Talks since 2010] promote debate. In fall 2017
our Disputaziuns Susch program held a conference around
the jubilee of the Reformation and its pivotal importance for
modern times. The Swiss reformer Huldrych Zwingli
attended the Disputaziuns 500 years ago in the church of
Susch where the future of Engadin's Reformation was
decided in 1537.

*What is your relationship with public or other institutions? Do you get
(public or private) funding?*

I believe it is the dialogue with friends and colleagues that
is most important in shaping the character of the museum.
Relationships with other institutions, both public and

private, are therefore essential to me. At the moment we are in discussion with Chus Martínez as we would be very interested in working together on a new institute for research on female art with the Art School in Basel. We very much appreciate the institutional landscape in which we are embedded, such as the Engadin Art Talks, the Bündner Kunstmuseum in Chur, the Ernst Ludwig Kirchner Museum in Davos, and the upcoming museum by Not Vital in Tarasp, to name just a few. Being situated in the Engadin it's crucial that we connect and coordinate all the initiatives. The museum is funded by my foundation. However, it is possible we will look for partnerships in the future.

In the past five years, what has been your greatest joy in running the museum? And what has been the biggest challenge?

My greatest joy has been the people I met and the team we built up along the journey to opening of the museum this year. The intensive process of forming a new project is always very stimulating for me. However, I find deeper satisfaction in the execution later on. When I spotted the abandoned brewery on the way to my home in Lower Engadin I had the idea that here the museum could come true. It is now very satisfying to see the idea transforming and turning into reality. It has been a great challenge to build within the existing structure of the old monastery. As I have learned before, historical structure may bring unexpected architectural solutions, which finally enrich the project. During the construction the architects and I have discovered tunnels and interconnections that are now restored and will serve as an internal exhibitional path in the museum.

What can a private museum do, that public institutions cannot? And what do you reply to people who criticize the proliferation of private museums?

Private museums do not replace public institutions, but rather enrich the institutional landscape. Whereas public institutions have to be very balanced and serve many different interests, private museums can be very special. For example, in my museum we focus on female artists.

I wouldn't see this combination coming from a public
institution. Public institutions are often trying to cover
the center. So in parallel to a certain canon it may construct,
a private museum can be more edgy and question it. Being
on the board of committees of big institutions such as the
Board for Eastern European Art at The Museum of Modern
Art, I really see the benefits and disadvantages from both
sides, and often I see special programmatic freedom within
private museums. Last but not least is a simplified decision
process.

*What are the greatest challenges in the long-term development of
a private museum? What are your plans for the next generation?*

The question is well put in that context, as long-term
development is as a matter of fact the greatest challenge for
private museums. I have given the museum a clear direction,
but how can I make sure that the museum will develop in
the same way without me? Aside from building up a trust-
worthy team, which I was talking about earlier, the board of
the foundation behind the museum becomes all-important.
With Jacqueline Burckhardt and Andrzej Przywara I believe
I have found a strong base with which to ensure the long-
term future of the museum, which captures its vision,
and will carry on the museum's mission even if the team
and circumstances change.

Do you have unrealized projects?

My unrealized projects are obviously the museum projects
like the Muzeum Art Stations at Stary Browar in Poznań
situated within the Stary Browar complex. The project
was developed ten years ago by Tadao Ando and was ready
to be executed. I had to terminate it due to insoluble issues
with the city council at that time.
     There is still one more project that cannot be
qualified as unrealized but rather as pending—it is project
for the future placement of my collection that I still dream
of being in Warsaw. I would like this project to be an
institutional venue where my art collection will be the
catalyst for future productions and art initiatives.

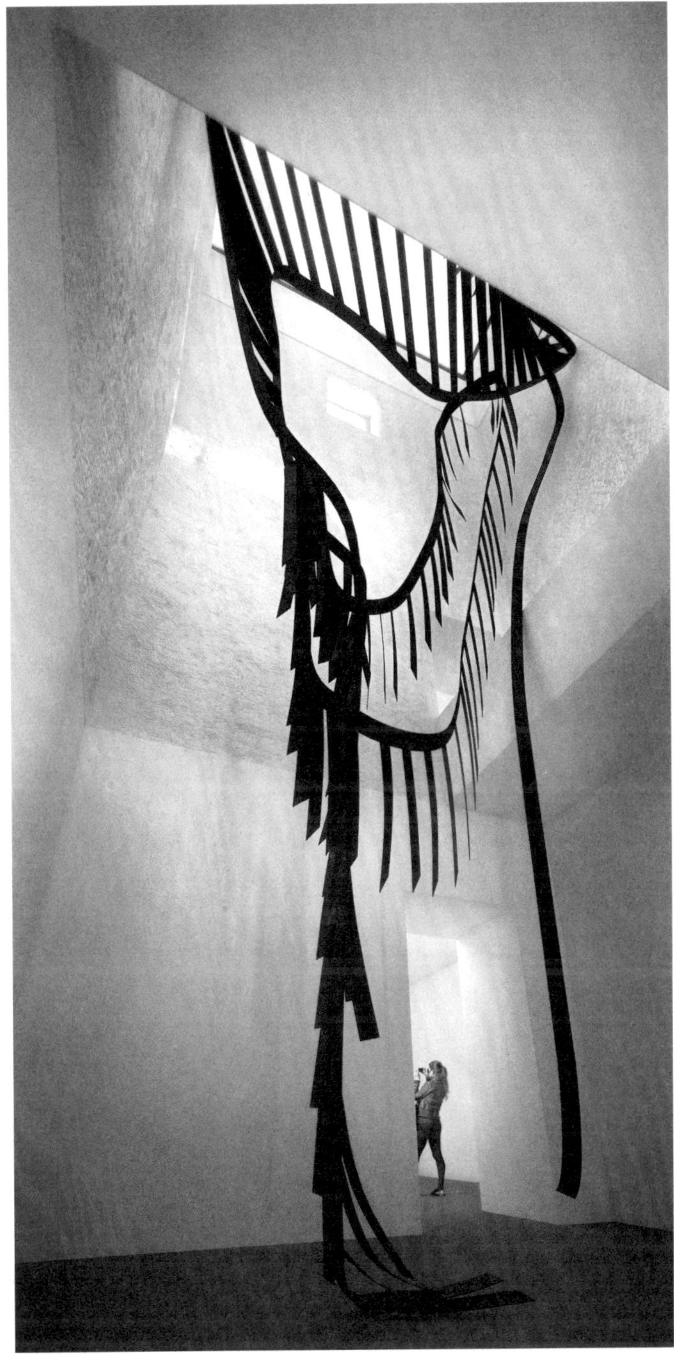

Rendered view of Muzeum Susch, Zernez, showing Monika Sosnowska's commission

Savina Lee
Savina Museum of Contemporary Art, Seoul

Savina Lee is director of the Savina Museum of Contemporary Art, which was established as the Savina Gallery in 1996, and registered as a museum in 2002. She is also the honorary president of the Korean Art Museum Association and Affiliated Professor in the Department of Fine Arts of Kookmin University.

Year of foundation: 2002
Size: 5-storey building
Number of employees: n/a
Visitors: n/a

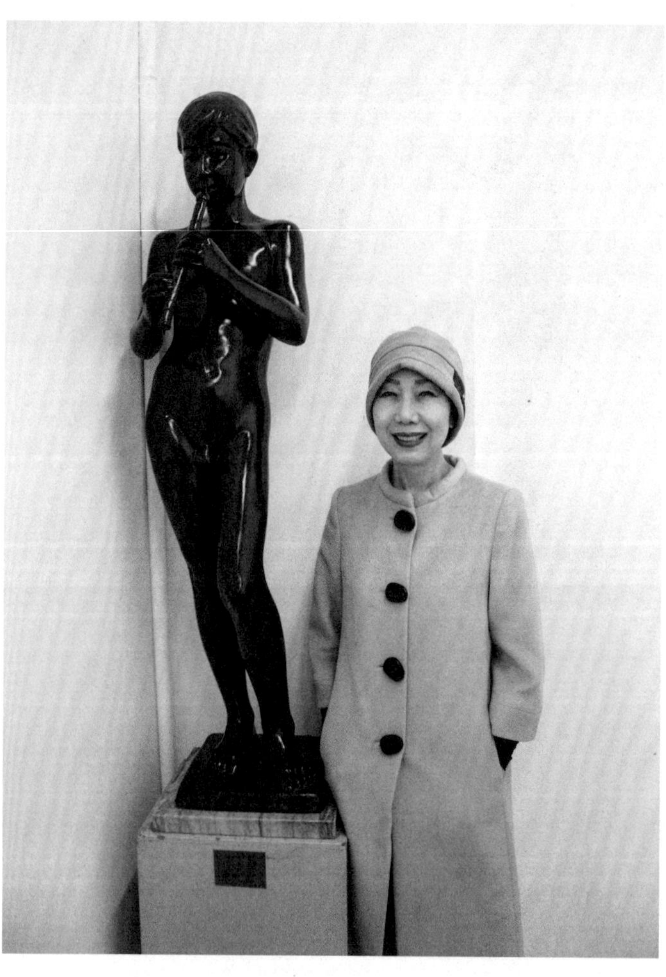

*What was your main motivation in
founding a museum?*

As an art enthusiast and curator,
I accumulated an art collection
naturally. It was hard to manage it
on an individual scale, so I began
to think about how to conserve
the collection in the long term.
And so I naturally decided to
found an art museum, a space
for exhibiting, conveying,
and holding artworks.

*What is the focus of your collection?
Do you concentrate on the presentation
of your collection or on organizing
temporary exhibitions?*

My art collections are based on
artistic value and originality.
I collect works of contemporary art
that are susceptible to be recorded
in the history of art. I focus
both on the collection and on
exhibitions.

How did you choose the location of the museum?

Accessibility via public transport was a priority in finding the right location. This allows audiences to visit more easily.

How did you choose the architect?

The present museum building was remodeled from an existing structure, but we will move the museum elsewhere in the future and commission an architect to design a new building.

How strongly are you involved in the running of the museum (programming, management, etc.)?

I am actively involved not only in programming and management, but also curating.

Do you have an educational program?

Yes, we have various education programs for adults and teenagers that accompany the exhibitions.

What is your relationship with public or other institutions?
Do you get (public or private) funding?

We apply for and receive public funding annually, but we hardly ever get private funding.

In the past five years, what has been your greatest joy in running the museum? What has been the biggest challenge?

The happiest memories in managing an art museum come from the moment when the exhibitions get great reviews from both critics and the public, or when the artists previously exhibited in the museum earn a good reputation. Apart from this we are faced with challenges, because a lot of people still have difficulties in distinguishing an art museum from a commercial art gallery. Due to the recent history of art museums here in comparison with the West, there are definitely obstacles to managing a nonprofit art museum.

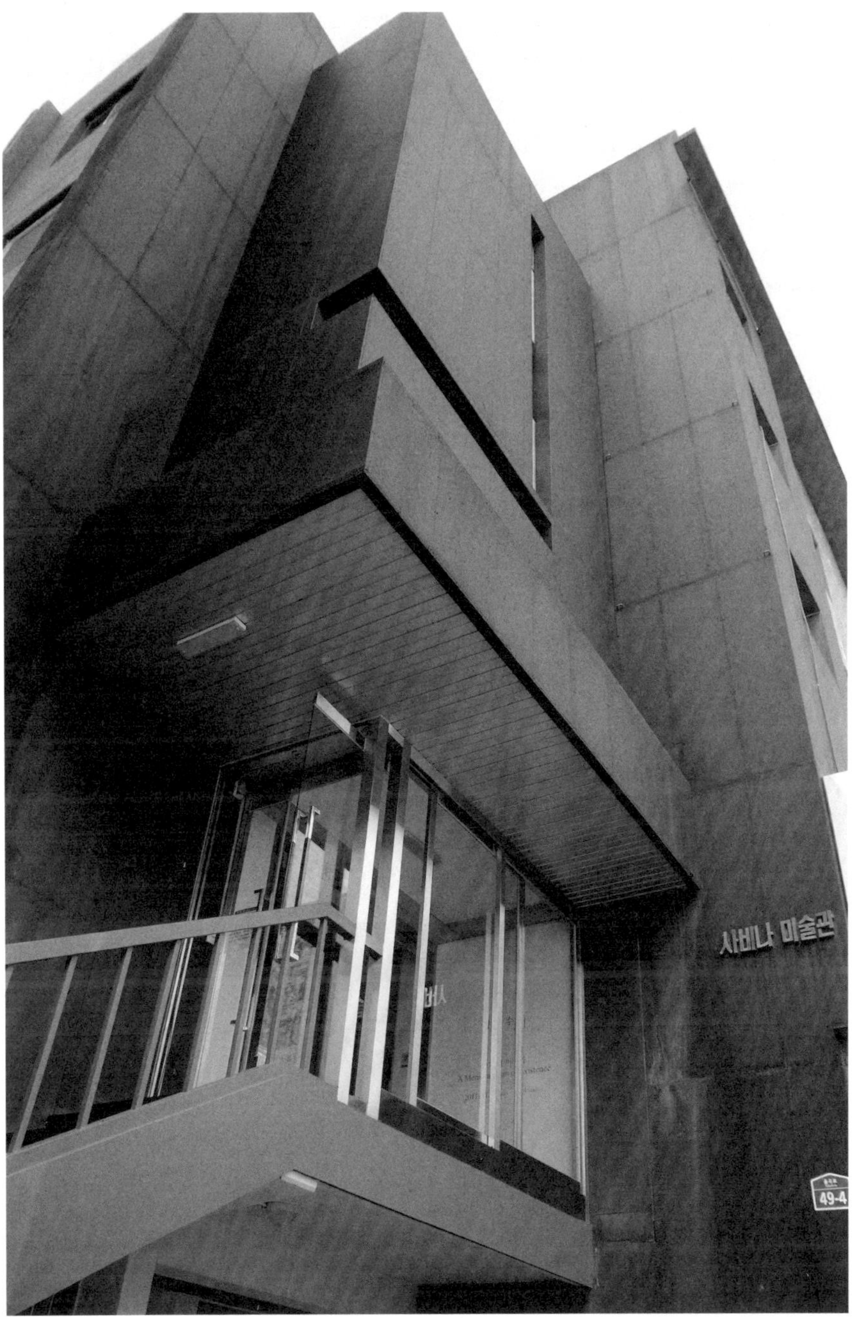

Savina Museum of Contemporary Art, Seoul

What can a private museum do, that public institutions cannot?
How do you respond to people who criticize the proliferation of
private museums?

Private art museums have a great deal of weight on the
Korean art scene. Based on statistics from 2016, private art
museums make up 70% of all the registered art museums,
which is 150 out of 219. Private art museums also hold more
attractive exhibitions than public art museums or blockbuster shows. Private art museums with independent
professional curators have successfully attracted large
audiences through different themes and audience-friendly
curating. Their collections are also very competitive
compared with public art museums.

What are the greatest challenges in the long-term development
of a private museum? What are your plans for the next generation?

The biggest challenge we face is the incorporation of private
art museums established by individuals into the public
system. We have often suggested to the government that
we would benefit from administrative support.

Eugenio López Alonso
Museo Jumex, Mexico City

Eugenio López Alonso created the Fundación Jumex Arte Contemporáneo, of which he has been the president since 2001. The foundation is supported by the Grupo Jumex, a fruit juice company founded by his father Eugenio López Rodea.

Year of foundation: 2013
Size: 6,700 m^2
Number of employees: n/a
Visitors: n/a

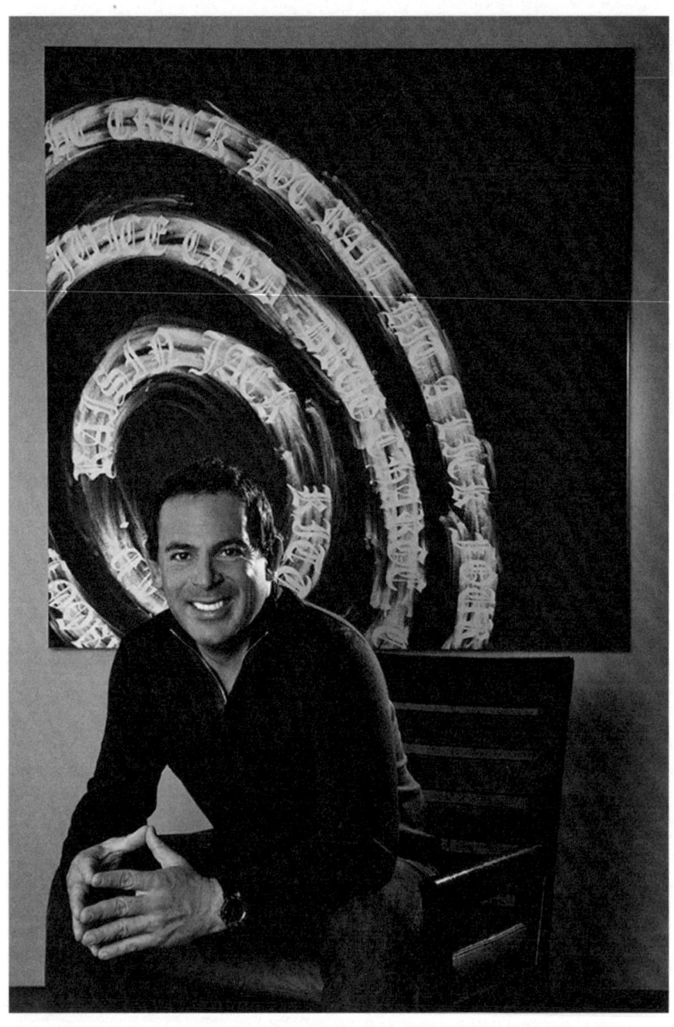

*What was your main motivation in
founding a museum?*

I have dreamed for a long time of
establishing a museum in Mexico
City that would enable local
audiences to experience contemporary art from around the world.
On my travels I have been inspired
by visiting many museums and
by seeing how important it is for
collectors to share with the public.
My hope for the Museo Jumex
is that it will engage audiences
in Mexico, and encourage their
appreciation of contemporary art.
I also hope that Museo Jumex
will show the world that Mexico
has a vibrant art scene of which
we can all be very proud.

*Did you have a specific model (i.e. an
existing collection) in mind, and is there
a tradition in your family of collecting
art?*

I am the first collector in my family.
Building a collection is a life-long

journey and, of course, one's taste continues to evolve based on life experiences.

When you aim to create an institution, you have to be more open-minded than when you buy for a private collection. You are confronted with a series of responsibilities, such as providing the public with information, and offering cultural references that will inspire their curiosity and expand their horizons. There are of course many remarkable institutions around the world that provide useful models for these functions, but we saw that Mexico City had its own specific needs.

What is the focus of your collection? Do you concentrate on the presentation of your collection or on organizing temporary exhibitions?

I began collecting artists who started working between 1980 and 1990.

When I started an international collection I was really hoping to bring it to Mexico—to open a space in my father's factory. I realized that if I could convince my father to make space for a collection in our warehouse then I would be able to buy big works of art. That's how everything started. At the same time I started to support young artists, to help them create their own projects.

We have made the collection available to the widest possible audience through exhibitions organized at Galería Jumex, formerly located in the grounds of the Jumex factory, and through a dynamic loan program with other institutions around the world.

Since the opening of Museo Jumex in 2013, the collection has reaffirmed its role as an important resource for the museum through temporary exhibitions.

How did you choose the location of the museum?

We wanted a location that would be accessible to as many people as possible. While we were conducting our research, an urban redevelopment program took on the restructuring of an obsolete industrial area on the outskirts of Polanco, which is a prestigious residential area. This initiative created an opportunity for us to become part of a new center being developed in the city.

How did you choose the architect?

When we began imagining a new museum, we visited many cultural institutions and interviewed many museum specialists. We then formulated a series of questions. What elements from existing museums should we embrace, and which should we avoid? What scale, what characteristics, what materials would be ideal for our vision? Vicente Todolí, the former director of Tate Modern [2002–2010], suggested that David Chipperfield could help us answer these questions. Once we visited his museums, the decision to work with him became extremely easy.

How strongly are you involved in the running of the museum (programming, management, etc.)?

As the founder of Fundación Jumex Arte Contemporáneo, I drive the vision of the institution. I'm fortunate to have the collaboration of an extraordinary team, led by Artistic Director Julieta González and Deputy Director Rosario Nadal.

Do you have an educational program?

Yes, absolutely. Through our education program, we aim to develop and strengthen the connections between ourselves, the artworks, and the community, above and beyond the links we create through our exhibitions.

What is your relationship with public or other institutions? Do you get (public or private) funding?

The museum does not receive public funding. We do collaborate with many local and international institutions to help us realize our mission. For example, we forge relationships with other institutions by lending works of art, and we benefit in turn when we work with our international colleagues to bring important exhibitions to Mexico City. In this way, our partnerships enable us to provide a more complete and diverse program.

*In the past five years, what has been your greatest joy in running
the museum? What has been the biggest challenge?*

My greatest joy has been to see how in only a couple of years
Museo Jumex has become an influential institution in
Mexico's cultural scene. As we continue to grow, we look
forward to expanding our education programs, as well
as curatorial and research initiatives that will help establish
the cultural base of future generations.

*What can a private museum do, that public institutions cannot?
How do you respond to people who criticize the proliferation of
private museums?*

It is hard to make sweeping statements, since each institution is different. For us, being a private institution has given
us the freedom to collect and build a unique international
contemporary art collection that can be shared with local
and international audiences.

In general, I think that private museums by their
nature benefit from greater independence. We are fortunate
to be able to bring our vision to fulfillment.

*What are the greatest challenges in the long-term development of
a private museum? What are your plans for the next generation?*

Museo Jumex opened just over four years ago, so we
continue to learn and evolve as we expand our programming.
We hope that our projects and exhibitions will contribute
positively to our local and regional communities as well
as internationally.

Do you have unrealized projects?

There are always dreams that I hope will one day come
to fruition.

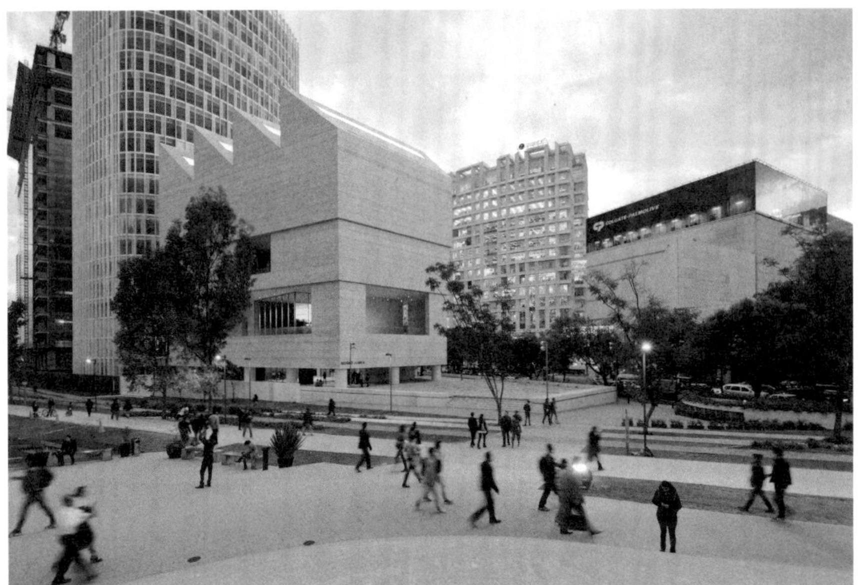

Museo Jumex, Mexico City

Philippe Méaille
Château de Montsoreau, Montsoreau

Philippe Méaille studied pharmacology in Paris. He has been collecting contemporary art since the 1990s and owns the most important ensemble of works by the artist collective Art & Language.

Year of foundation: 2016
Size: n/a
Number of employees: n/a
Visitors: n/a

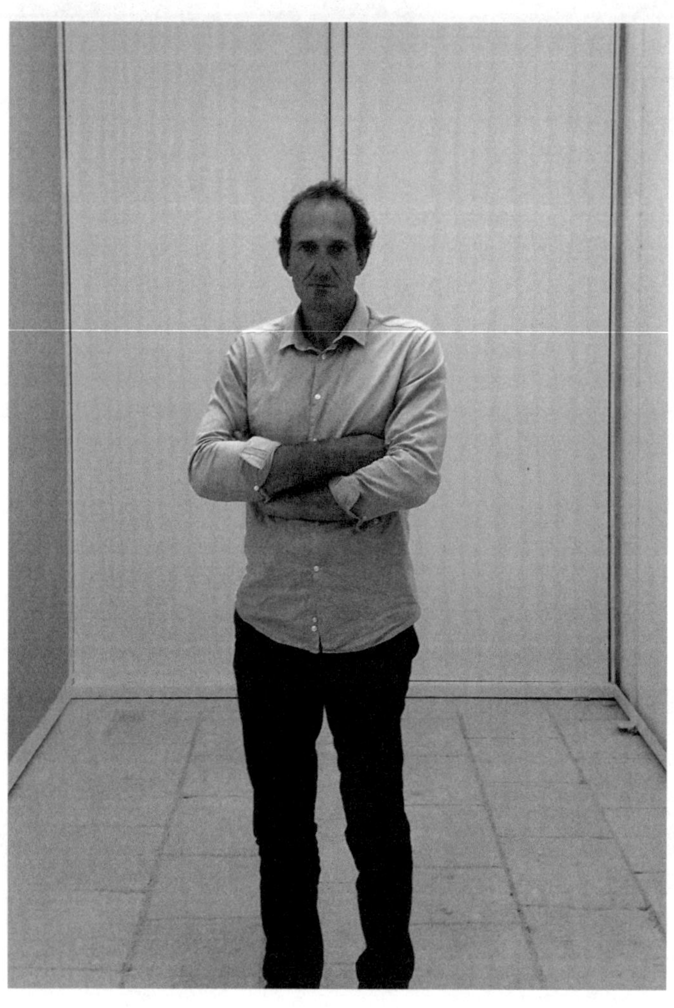

*What was your main motivation in
founding a museum?*

There are a lot of good reasons for
founding a museum: the desire to
share a private passion or the need
to realize an educational purpose,
for example. Our collection is
focused on works by the pioneering
artists Art & Language, who
invented Conceptual art in the
1960s. By questioning the art practices of modernism they sought
to reintegrate the viewer into
the creation of the art object. Their
work has been very influential in
the wider artistic field, and most
critics date the beginning of what
is now called "contemporary art"
to that moment. When I was 20 or
21, I bought a work from 1965 called
Mirror Piece and installed it in my
apartment in Paris. After two or
three days, I felt very sad and stupid
because I understood the limit
imposed if these works were kept
private. They would be like a
discussion that was kept secret.

Therefore I felt a responsibility to make this collection accessible to the widest possible public.

Did you have a specific model (i.e. an existing collection) in mind, and is there a tradition in your family of collecting art?

Yes, both my parents collected art and I have been going to auction houses since my childhood. I don't really know if you are able as a child to make out the difference between what is called a "collection" and the content of an entire art auction. I would say that I have been more impressed by certain çollectors than by an existing collection. Myriam and Jacques Salomon in France, and Eric Fabre in Belgium are significant among the collectors who have impressed me.

What is the focus of your collection? Do you concentrate on the presentation of your collection or on organizing temporary exhibition?

The artists of Art & Language have often characterized their works as "homeless stuff," so I am trying to give them a home. Conceptual art brought instability to the art object and has been more focused on a practice than on a consumable product. That is what we are trying to show at the Château de Montsoreau. We look through the lens of this revolution in building temporary exhibitions. It is a revolution that represents the last big adventure in art.

How did you choose the location of the museum and the architect?

I have settled the museum in a Château of the Loire. I wanted the museum to be both in France and in an international context. There are many international destinations in France: among them we have Paris, we have the Côte d'Azur, and we have the Châteaux of the Loire. I wanted the museum to be in a settled residential location and to give a clear message to the visitors that they are welcome to take their time. The Château de Montsoreau is itself fascinating, because of its history, its location, and its connection with artists like William Turner, Auguste Rodin, and Alexandre Dumas. It is the first and indeed the only château to have been built into the riverbed of the Loire. It combines radical Renaissance architecture with a dramatic presence in the natural landscape.

*How strongly are you involved in the running of the museum
(programming, management, etc.)?*

Our museum is based on a collection of Art & Language
works that I have acquired over the last 25 years. I have,
therefore, a good knowledge of this collection personally.
We have a sort of an institutional responsibility: we are,
in effect, institutionalizing something that is highly resistant
to such a condition. Our goal is thus to share a discussion
with our visitors rather than to give them an experience
as passive cultural consumers. This is where I am involved.

Do you have an educational program?

Our educational program is based on that discussion.
There is not one truth to be found in or about the work,
no univocal interpretation. Art is something that we build
together in a discussion that is both playful and very serious.
We first want our visitors to take pleasure in this activity.

*What is your relationship with public or other institutions? Do you get
(public or private) funding?*

A big part of our energy is still dedicated to establishing
a selected network of institutions, to help them become
involved with Art & Language. The Philippe Méaille
Collection has been on loan to MACBA in Barcelona since
2010; MACBA has, since its beginnings, been very close to
Conceptual art and has also created a very strong audience
for Art & Language. We can learn from that experience.
       We receive public funding for our temporary
exhibitions.

*In the past five years, what has been your greatest joy in running
the museum? What has been the biggest challenge?*

Formally the works of Art & Language are not stable; they
can be a piece of paper, an installation, a collection of
photographs, music, a video, or painting. We are still learning
about our building, and we are also learning from our visitors,
because the place is dedicated to them. Every installation of
an Art & Language work is both a great challenge and a great

joy for that reason. We opened in 2016, with a performance
by The Jackson Pollock Bar, who produce what they call
Theory Installations, where actors perform by lip-synching
a theoretical text that has been prerecorded by other voices.

For our opening, they performed *An Interview with
Victorine Meurent*—a text written by Art & Language. It was
a great joy to have the performance at the Château.

*What can a private museum do, that public institutions cannot?
How do you respond to people who criticize the proliferation of
private museums?*

We do not. We can do nothing more than they can. However,
we can offer a distinctive view of what is important: we can
be slow, we can take our time to decide what to show,
and we can take time to talk to people. I have a lot of respect
for the Palais de Tokyo and Tate Modern. They represent
two different ways to bring art to visitors, and they are doing
it in the best way possible. There is, however, an antagonism
involved. We are running a museum here because we have
successfully built a collection, and because the works demand
to be in a public sphere; we don't want to offend anybody.

*What are the greatest challenges in the long-term development of
a private museum? What are your plans for the next generation?*

The Internet is the biggest site of exchange, of discussion,
and maybe soon of content. Museums are about experiencing
the world physically. Our greatest challenge is to make
the museum not only a place of exchange, of discussion,
and creation for an audience and network that already exist,
but also to do this through the Internet. We need to link
the virtual world with the physical world and to think about
a discussion on the scale that implies.

Do you have unrealized projects?

I have many unrealized projects: one of them would be to
build an extension to the Château de Montsoreau so as to be
able to show more of the collection. It would be a great
challenge as the Château has been listed since 1862 and it is
located in a UNESCO World Heritage site.

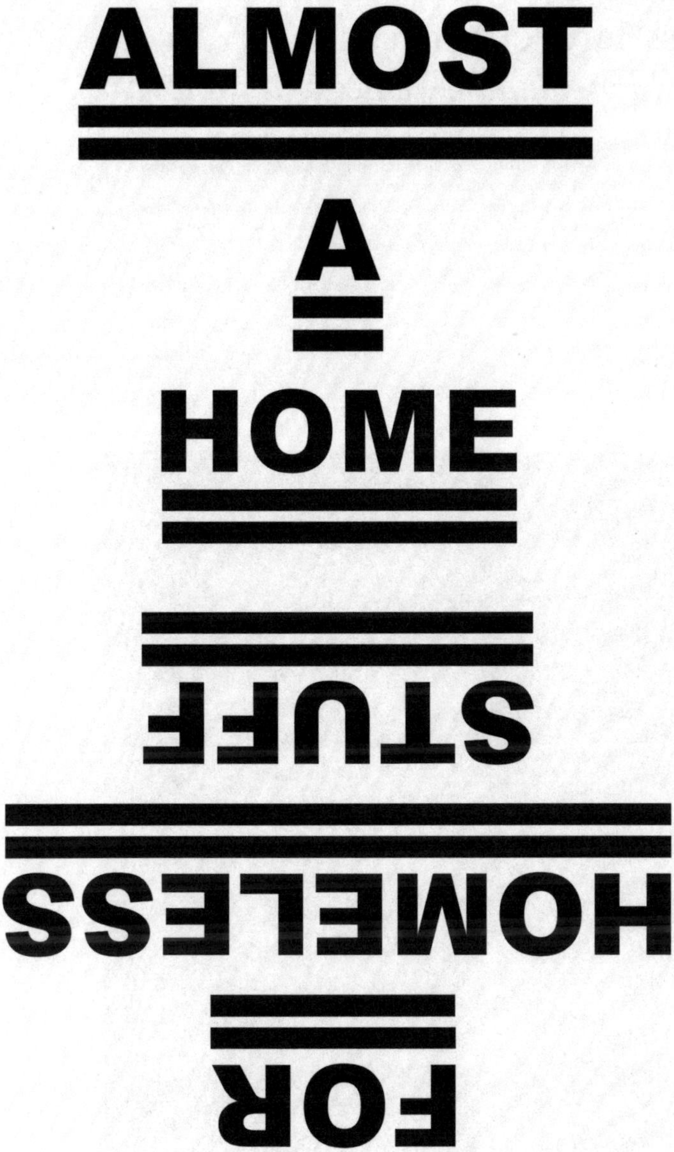

ALMOST

A
=
HOME

STUFF

HOMELESS

FOR

Art & Language, *Almost a Home for Homeless Stuff*, 2017

Leonid Mikhelson and Teresa Iarocci Mavica
V-A-C Foundation, Venice and Moscow

Leonid Mikhelson studied civil engineering, and is CEO and a major shareholder of the Russian independent gas company Novatek. He is an art collector, patron, and founder and president of the V-A-C Foundation, which was established in 2009.

    Teresa Iarocci Mavica studied political science and has long worked in the arts in Russia. After setting up an experimental platform for young artists and curators, she was invited by Leonid Mikhelson to set up and direct the V-A-C Foundation.

Year of foundation: 2009 (foundation); 2017 (first permanent space and learning space in Venice); 2019 (completion date for the GES2 Museum, Moscow)
Size: n/a
Number of employees: n/a
Visitors: n/a

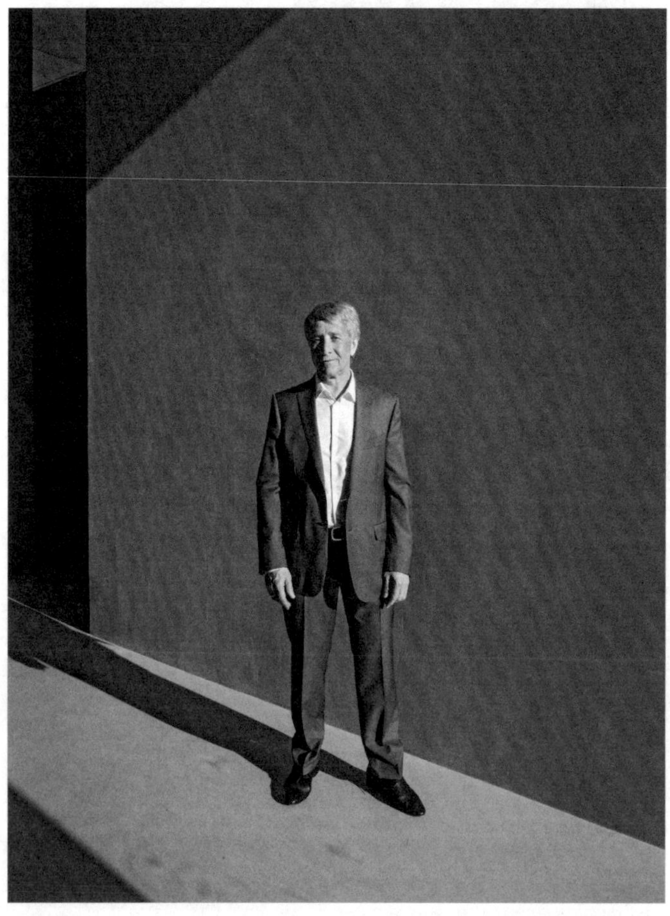

What was your main motivation in founding a museum?

TIM The story behind V-A-C Foundation is one of a collector whose passion for the arts led him to become more actively involved as a patron and subsequently as founder and president of the V-A-C Foundation. We share a strong sense of commitment to the new generations living, studying, and working in Russia. We want to create new platforms, bring people closer to art, and encourage their involvement in producing new culture together.

Did you have a specific model (i.e. an existing collection) in mind, and is there a tradition in your family of collecting art?

LM No, I don't have any specific models. The collection for me, on a personal level, is a journey through the history of art, as it hopefully is and will continue to be for all those

working with it. My ambition is to create new models, and it
is for this very reason that the collection does not follow a
traditional development, but reflects more on the strategies
created by the Foundation.

*What is the focus of your collection? Do you concentrate on
the presentation of your collection or on organizing temporary
exhibitions?*

LM/TIM   While individual works have been included in a
variety of exhibitions, our focus has always been much
broader than simply presenting the collection. Cultural
production is central to our activity, as is establishing new
cross-cultural dialogues and creating alternative settings
and platforms for bringing different artistic practices
together. We have an annual calendar of temporary group
and solo exhibition projects, performances, and events on
an international, national, and local scale.

The V-A-C collection is a constantly developing body
of works including sculpture, installation, painting, photog-
raphy, film, and performance from artists such as Francis
Bacon, Liz Deschenes, Alighiero Boetti, Wade Guyton,
Wassily Kandinsky, Lucy McKenzie, Amedeo Modigliani,
Mike Nelson, Gerhard Richter, Bridget Riley, James
Richards, Dayanita Singh, and Christopher Wool. One could
say that the collection explores the inner and outer borders
of the avant-gardes through time, where a seminal work by
Natalia Goncharova can be placed in dialogue with a work by
Hito Steyerl, for example. The collection also reflects the
path that the Foundation has taken since its inception.
When we open our future home, GES2, we want to share the
collection with our visitors, and plan to include it in certain
aspects of the program.

How did you choose the location of the museum?

LM/TIM   Originally a power station, GES2 was built on the
banks of the Moskva River between 1904 and 1907. We were
interested in the preservation of prerevolutionary architecture in Moscow and working with an existing structure that
is an integral part of the landscape. When we first saw it,
the power station was already scheduled to be closed down

entirely, and could have easily ended up an industrial relic, abandoned. GES2 is a remarkable building, and as soon as we saw it we knew it belonged back in the public realm. The building is also very central, situated in the iconic Red October District, where the redbrick Krasny Oktyabr chocolate factory once stood. The renowned Strelka Institute and the historic Udarnik Theatre are also in the neighborhood.

How did you choose the architect?

TIM　As our aim was to retrieve the GES2 power station and create a space for the public, we had no doubt in our minds that the architect had to be Renzo Piano. Designing true living spaces is central to his work. The Centre Pompidou is just one example of how Piano brought the city inside the museum, while also making it an immediate and integral part of the city. Also, Italian architecture had a strong influence on prerevolutionary Russia, and we wanted to bring that back somehow.

How strongly are you involved in the running of the museum (programming, management, etc.)?

LM　Despite the fact that my work is extremely demanding, I strive to remain actively engaged in the strategic development of the V-A-C Foundation, and to be present as much as possible. Teresa Iarocci Mavica, Victoria Mikhelson, and I make decisions together about the Foundation. We are also fortunate to have Francesco Manacorda as our artistic director, and a talented team of young Moscow-based curators, who are constantly working on new ideas and generating an experimental program.

Do you have an educational program?

TIM　An extensive learning program already forms an integral part of V-A-C's activities. We have an ongoing series of talks, discussions, film screenings, and workshops, encouraging open conversation and debate around our exhibitions and artist's projects. Moving forward, we aim to create new learning models, to produce new culture and content together with artists and, above all, with our audiences.

What is your relationship with public or other institutions? Do you get (public or private) funding?

TIM/LM   We have no public funding. The V-A-C Foundation is a nonprofit, private institution. We work with and enjoy long-standing collaborations and partnerships with museums around the world, from the Whitechapel Gallery and Tate Gallery in London to M HKA (Museum of Contemporary Art) in Antwerp, and the Art Institute of Chicago. We are currently working with the Paris- and San Francisco-based Kadist Foundation and with the Moscow Museum of Modern Art on multi-layered exhibition projects combining our collections. Collaboration with other institutions both in Russia and abroad has been and will always be central to our work in opening Russia up to the wider world through the arts.

In the past five years, what has been your greatest joy in running the foundation? What has been the biggest challenge?

LM/TIM   As we approach our first ten-year anniversary (in 2019), the greatest joy without a doubt is seeing the fruits of our labor, as increasing numbers of young Russian artists are being invited to participate in international exhibitions. From projects in Moscow and around the world, to the opening of our new space in Venice in 2017, the work of the V-A-C Foundation has grown larger in scope and ambition. We have now reached a pivotal moment as we prepare for the opening of GES2, certainly our biggest challenge yet.

What can a private museum do, that public institutions cannot? How do you respond to people who criticize the proliferation of private museums?

TM   A private museum, if based on genuine initiative and the will to interact with the public and not as a showcase or—even worse—for personal gain, can be an incredible asset to society. There are advantages to the ways private spaces can engage the public, more informally, more

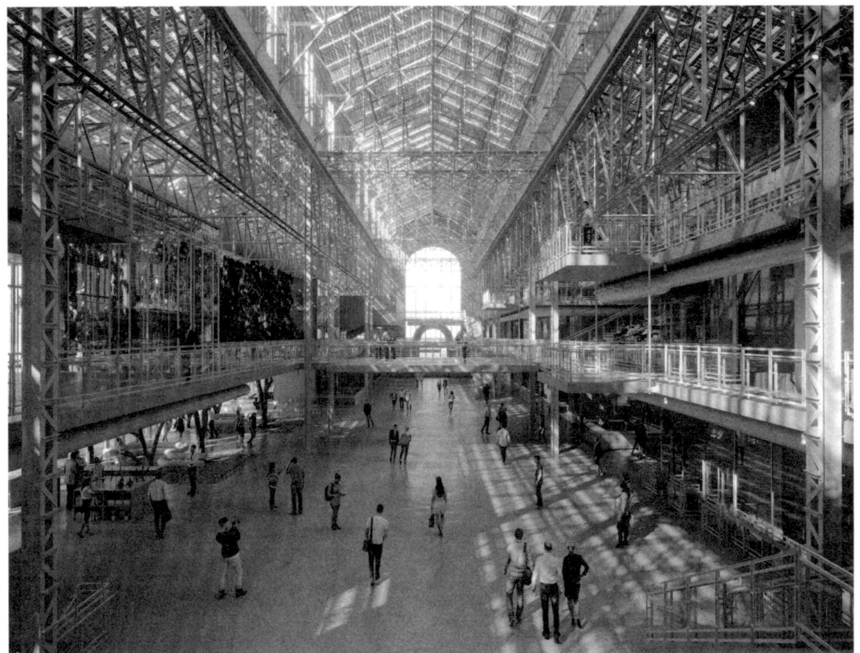

Rendered view of the GES2 Museum, V-A-C Foundation, Moscow

independently and experimentally than public institutions. Criticizing the proliferation of private museums surely means criticizing the proliferation of culture. Maybe not all private museums out there are significant, but this also goes for public museums. We can never learn enough, and if a private individual wants to contribute to that then they should be able to do so. Society and history will be the ones to judge their work.

What are the greatest challenges in the long-term development of a private museum? What are your plans for the next generation?

LM/TIM   In Russia today, the concept of a "private museum" is still not recognized in law. Although the V-A-C Foundation is a private, nonprofit project, it is still categorized as a commercial exercise. This is part of the country's legacy, its history, and our challenge is to change this approach so that the role of the private sector is recognized. In this country, today, it is about acknowledging and making the individual a focus of attention once again. It means a lot more than opening a museum.

Do you have unrealized projects?

LM   Luckily yes, and thankfully I still have time to realize them.

Judith Neilson
White Rabbit Collection, Sydney

Judith Neilson trained as a graphic designer. She is founder and director of the White Rabbit Gallery in Sydney, which is home to one of the world's largest collections of contemporary Chinese art. She is a stakeholder of Platinum Asset Management, founded in 1994 by Kerr Neilson, her former husband.

Year of foundation: 2001 (Gallery opening: 2009)
Size: n/a
Number of employees: n/a
Visitors: n/a

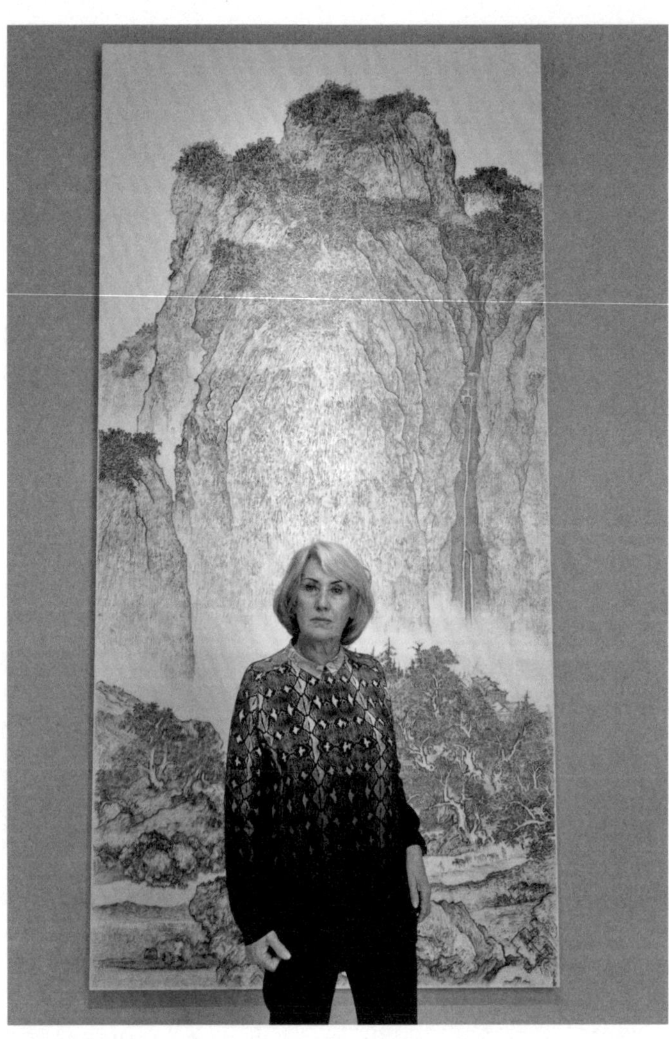

What was your main motivation in founding a museum?

I was in a position where I could spend time sourcing artworks by artists I admired who were not necessarily commercial "names." I wanted to share these works with a public who would enjoy them and who were keen to see and learn about something new.

Did you have a specific model (i.e. an existing collection) in mind, and is there a tradition in your family of collecting art?

I have always been a collector of art. In the White Rabbit Collection and in the White Rabbit Gallery, I did not follow specific models. They both emerged from my vision. There has been a lot of learning along the way, but I now have an incredible team who all want White Rabbit to be the best.

*What is the focus of your collection? Do you concentrate on
the presentation of your collection or on organizing temporary
exhibitions?*

The focus of my collection is on Chinese contemporary art
since 2000. Many of the artworks have a global character
and are not readily identifiable as Chinese. The White Rabbit
Gallery exhibits only works drawn from the collection.
Exhibitions run for five months and are usually inspired by
a particular theme. Between exhibitions we spend four
or five weeks deinstalling and installing.

How did you choose the location of the museum?

It needed to be near the city center and be easily accessible
by public transport. The White Rabbit Gallery is located in
an old building just south of central Sydney, near the main
railway station.

How did you choose the architect?

The building needed to be completely refurbished.
The architectural firm was recommended to me.

*How strongly are you involved in the running of the museum
(programming, management, etc.)?*

I am the owner of the White Rabbit Collection and the
unique funder of the Gallery. I have the final say in everything. I have an office in the Gallery building and visit it
daily.

Do you have an educational program?

The White Rabbit Gallery did have an educational program—
teachers would bring their classes and we would provide
tailored tours for them. I recently stopped this, because as
overall visitor numbers soared, the large groups were taking
a toll on the Gallery building and facilities. Many students
continue to visit the Gallery and its library, but they come
in as individuals. The Gallery runs two public tours each day,
and these are very informative and very popular.

What is your relationship with public or other institutions? Do you get (public or private) funding?

I have a good relationship with other art museums and institutions such as the Sydney Biennale. I have loaned works from the White Rabbit Collection to public museums around Australia. White Rabbit welcomes scholars of Chinese art, and we are the only place that holds substantial information on many Chinese contemporary artists. I provide all the funds needed to operate the Gallery and I don't receive any outside funding.

In the past five years, what has been your greatest joy in running the museum? What has been the biggest challenge?

It has been wonderful to see the staff and our visitors mature and become more knowledgeable about Chinese contemporary art. At the White Rabbit Gallery, all the staff have a sense of ownership. We all want it to be the best museum of its kind.

What can a private museum do, that public institutions cannot? How do you respond to people who criticize the proliferation of private museums?

I do not understand why anyone would criticize private museums. I wonder how many of those who level such criticism contribute funds to museums themselves.

Most private museums are open to the general public and charge minimal or no admission fees. Their relatively small size and frequent exhibition changes allow audiences to experience works that in a public museum might lie in a vault for decades. Many public museums also lack the funding for state-of-the-art conservation and storage, so their works are not always cared for as well as those in private museums. Even donated artworks can be costly for public museums to accept because they have to be documented and properly housed. I do not know of any private museum owner/collector who has refused to loan or donate works to other museums. In such cases, it is the private owner who bears most of the costs.

In private museums, a single collector usually chooses the works on show. This provides a consistency that may be lacking in public museums, and it makes private museums more accessible and user-friendly. Unlike most public museums, private museums are not subject to content controls, censorship, and financial or bureaucratic constraints. Curators in public institutions may see an artwork as important, but lack the funds to acquire it or have to await approval from a board or committee. Private collectors are in a better position to act quickly, so they can often obtain pieces before public museums make a move.

What are the greatest challenges in the long-term development of a private museum? What are your plans for the next generation?

There is always room for improvement, and with information technology advancing rapidly, it is important to try to be prepared and keep an open mind. The past 17 years have been transformative. Invention, inspiration, and imitation have changed and multiplied in ways that no one in 2000 could have foreseen.

Do you have unrealized projects?

Storage and documentation of every piece is my main concern right now. At the end of 2017, I will be moving the White Rabbit Collection into a state-of-the-art building (entirely separate from the Gallery) with curatorial offices and storage space, conservation and photography facilities, a library and research center, and a performance space. This will be open by invitation or request.

I consider my collection a document, not a "star show." I hope it will prove valuable as a historical record, but I have no idea which works will be judged "great" decades from now. Many artists have fallen in and out of favor and fashion since I began the White Rabbit Collection, and I don't believe I am in a position to predict the future. Because of that, I collect according to my own eye and inclinations.

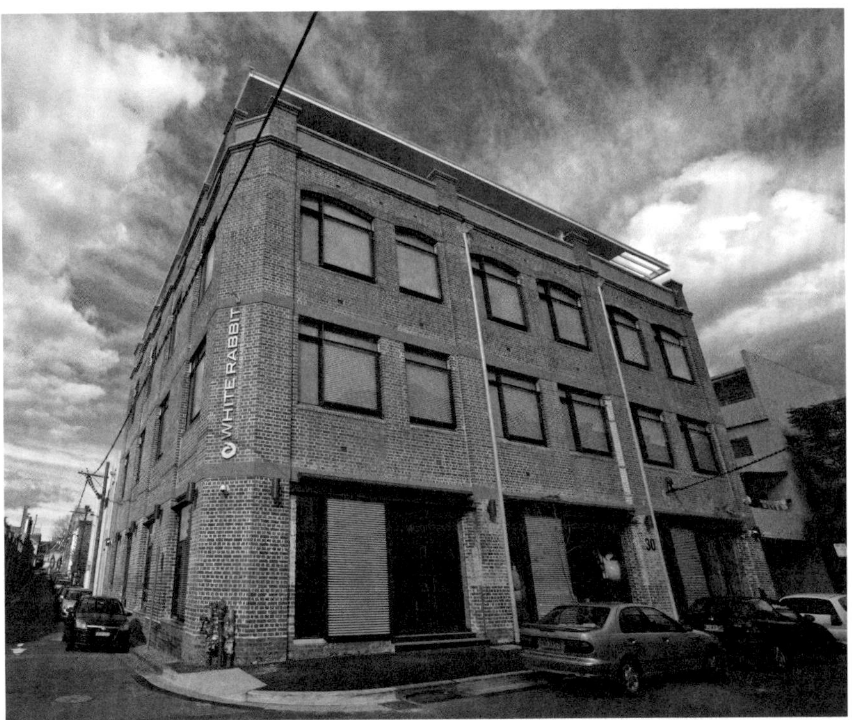

White Rabbit Gallery, Sydney

Bernardo Paz
Instituto Inhotim, Brumadinho

Bernardo Paz is a mining and steelmaking entrepreneur. He joined the Itaminas group in 1973 and made it one of the most important mining and steelmaking corporations in Minas Gerais, Brazil, with a domestic and international market. In 1988 he initiated the Instituto Inhotim.

Year of foundation: 2006
Size: 140 hectares
Number of employees: 500 +
Visitors: c. 300,000 a year

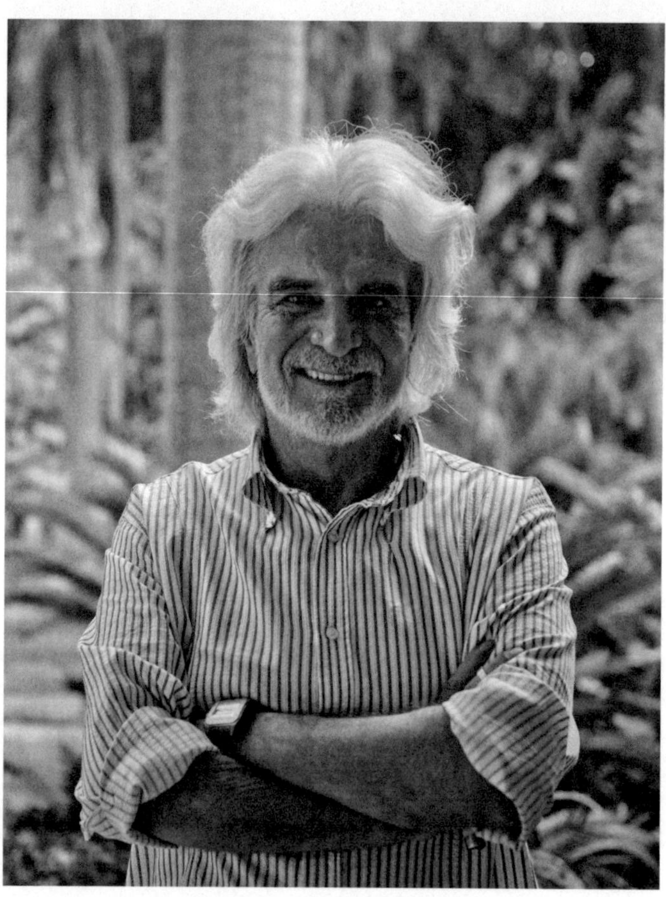

What was your main motivation in founding a museum?

Beauty and curiosity. This is related to my DNA. My mother liked poetry and painting and my father was an engineer and also worked on some architectural projects. At the age of 22, I started working in mining. I was directing several companies, but at the same time I was dreaming of a little house and a hammock. After many years of working in this field, I bought a small farm in Brumadinho, close to Belo Horizonte, in the state of Minas Gerais. In the 1980s I started to create the garden— this is where the beauty is really found. Then I couldn't see the point of having the garden just for itself, so I started building some pavilions to display works of art. Over the years, the Institute became unanimously appreciated. Among the more than 2.5 million visitors we have had, 99% think they have lived a dream in Inhotim.

It's not just art, just botany. Inhotim is a state of mind.

Did you have a specific model (i.e. an existing collection) in mind, and is there a tradition in your family of collecting art?

Inhotim was created in an intuitive way. I had a modern art collection, and, influenced by the Brazilian artist Tunga, I decided to shift the collection to contemporary art. Over time, I began to understand that what we were putting together went beyond the nature of individual ownership. The combination of nature and the art collection had a cultural value that should be an asset available to everyone. I have always been devoted to art as the foundation of culture and life. I am passionate about culture in general. All cultural shows interest me, even when one accepts culture as technology. I am an ordinary person, born in a simple family, who, somehow, created something good for the world.

What is the focus of your collection? Do you focus on the presentation of your collection or on organizing temporary exhibitions?

The collection is not mine anymore. It was all donated to Inhotim, which is a private nonprofit entity qualified by the government of Minas Gerais and by the federal government as a Public Interest Civil Society Organization (Oscip). Accumulation is one thing I've always fought against. That is not my purpose, or the purpose of Inhotim. The mission of the Institute is social. Inhotim's collection features paintings, sculptures, drawings, photographs, videos, and installations by over 250 renowned Brazilian and international artists from 30 countries. The collection comprises over 1,300 works, 700 of which are currently on display. Inhotim has 23 pavilions (19 permanent, and four dedicated to temporary exhibitions). The diversity is what makes the collection so distinct. Some of the highlights are the permanently installed works by Adriana Varejão, Chris Burden, Cildo Meireles, Claudia Andujar, Hélio Oiticica, Lygia Pape, and Tunga.

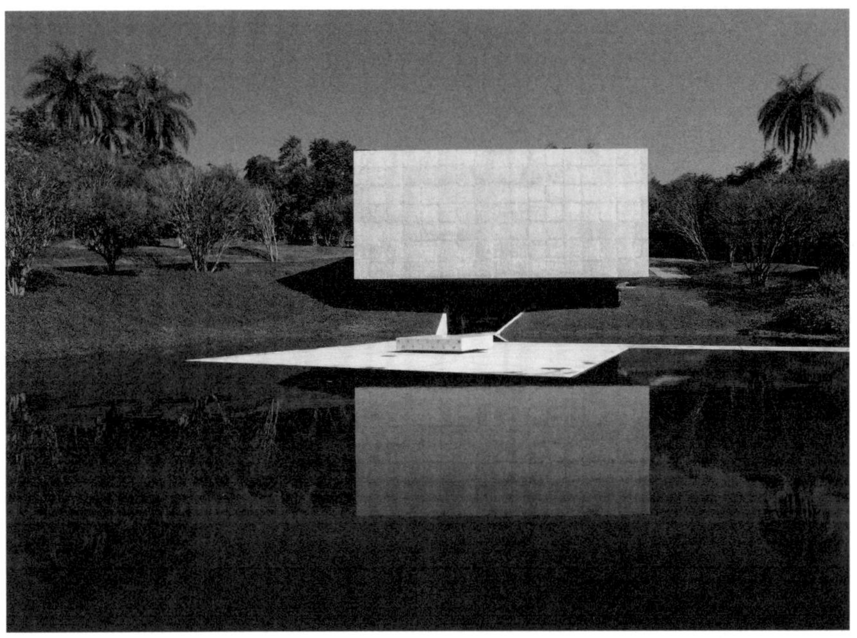

Galeria Adriana Varejão, Instituto Inhotim, Brumadinho

How did you choose the location of the museum?

I was born in Belo Horizonte and I built part of my professional trajectory in mining. I could have created Inhotim
in São Paulo, for example. However, for me it was important
to return to where I came from, where I intend to stay,
and to develop this process. Inhotim is located in a mining
area, at the division of two Brazilian biomes. The Institute
has provided alternative employment opportunities, and has
become a place of leisure, and a place for those seeking
contact with art and nature. Luckily, this place has become
something unique, and attracts worldwide interest.

How did you choose the architect?

In Inhotim, architecture is at the service of the works of art
on display. The artworks are the starting point for creating
a dialogue between art and architecture. In this sense,
Inhotim differs from many of the great museums in which
imposing buildings are occupied by works of art. When
working with the equation art-architecture-landscape,
we managed to construct buildings like those that house
works by Claudia Andujar, Lygia Pape, and Adriana Varejão.
From the beginning, the institution opted for young
architects, bringing new voices to the area. This choice
contrasts with the history of the architecture of Minas Gerais,
known for the works by great names like that of the
architect Oscar Niemeyer.

How strongly are you involved in the running of the museum?

I'm a supervisor. I always try to work with people who
understand the field much more than I do. Today these
people are employees of Inhotim. At the beginning, before
the Institute was open to the public, I had to manage all
alone, with the support of my friends Roberto Burle Marx
and Tunga. Today, Inhotim has about 500 employees.
We also have an international curatorial team, who take care
of our art collection, and new projects and exhibitions.

Do you have an educational program?

About 2,500 students from public and private schools in Brumadinho and Belo Horizonte Metropolitan Area visit Inhotim every week. The educational programs of Inhotim promote a number of actions to bring society closer to values related to art, the environment, community empowerment, and cultural diversity. In addition to the partnerships with schools, city halls, and city and state education departments, the Institute also offers free educational guided visits to the public in general in order to provide a context for visitors who wish to know more about what the park offers in terms of contemporary art, botany, and environment.

What is your relationship with public or other institutions? Do you get (public or private) funding?

Inhotim is my life. I try to be present and engage with the visitors. I am in the park almost every day, despite having other jobs and companies. The public is as important as the big companies that fund us. What brings me satisfaction is to observe the reactions and emotions that the Inhotim experience provides to the visitors. In Brazil, we have the Rouanet Law, which stimulates culture. This allows us a series of partnerships, and gives us credibility in order to obtain public and private funding. It is also very important for Inhotim that the public engages with this type of initiative.

In the past five years, what has been your greatest joy in running the museum? What has been the biggest challenge?

My life has been always a challenge. Sometimes we are surprised by the news that Inhotim received more than 13,000 people in a single day. One of the things that excites me is the unanimous acceptation of Inhotim in Brazil and the world. It makes me happy.

*What can a private museum do, that public institutions cannot?
How do you respond to people who criticize the proliferation of
private museums?*

At Inhotim, artists have the opportunity to develop the best
works of their lives. The Institute gives them the conditions
and freedom to create. There are several private museums,
which are good for artists to show their work to a multitude
of people. What I condemn is someone who accumulates
works just for speculation. It is commendable that there are
both private and public museums, that art can develop in
every environment.

*What are the greatest challenges in the long-term development of
a private museum? What are your plans for the next generation?*

Inhotim began in a personal way at first. Then it became
a center for contemporary art and a botanical garden visited
by more than 300,000 people from all over the world per
year. The challenges for me have arisen become day by day.
I like the curious and critical art inside the park that turns
it into something never seen before. I hope that in the next
few years I will find someone who understands the philosophy of the place, and can continue its work for the next
generation.

Do you have unrealized projects?

We are negotiating the construction of viaducts, roads,
a private airport 10 minutes away that will be called Inhotim.
Additional hotels are already being constructed in the park.
This leads us to believe that Inhotim can receive various
models of art festival, and events involving ballet, intelli-
gence, nanotechnology, among other areas of knowledge.

Editors' Note
Bernardo Paz was sentenced for tax evasion in November 2017, several months after this interview
was conducted. What will happen to Inhotim is still unresolved, but we decided to include the
interview as Inhotim remains an important example of a private museum initiative.

Lekha Poddar
Devi Art Foundation, New Delhi

Lekha Poddar comes from an Indian industrialist family and began collecting art in the 1980s. In 2008 she founded the Devi Art Foundation with her younger son Anupam.

Year of foundation: 2008
Size: nomadic
Number of employees: 5
Visitors: c. 10,000 people per exhibition

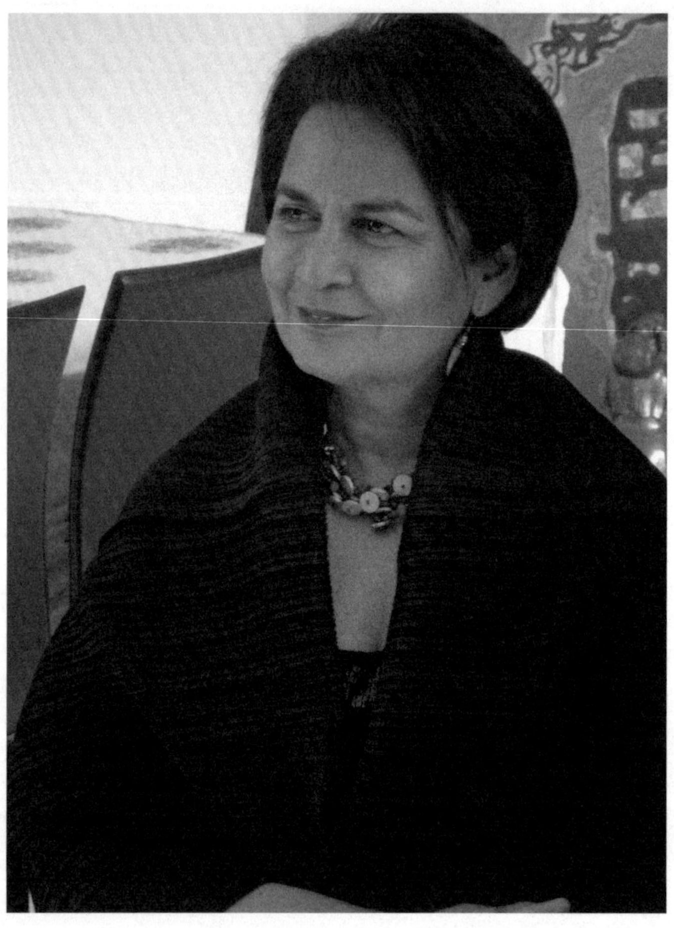

What was your main motivation in founding a museum?

In the late 1990s, my son Anupam and I were about the only collectors of Indian contemporary art. Most people from abroad who were interested in Indian contemporary art—museum directors, collectors, gallerists—were usually directed to our home. Slowly we realized that what we were collecting was important. In 2005 my husband Ranjan Poddar was constructing a new office building. He was not using the entire space and agreed to give us about 750 square meters to use for our collection. We debated whether to create a museum or a foundation. Ultimately we settled for the latter.

We opened doors of Devi Art Foundation in August 2008. Since we already had a collection our main aim was to give young people from different art backgrounds a chance to curate cutting edge shows.

*Did you have a specific model (i.e. an existing collection) in mind,
and is there a tradition in your family of collecting art?*

We did not have any model in mind nor was there any
tradition of collecting in the family. Our sole purpose with
the foundation was to give a platform to young non-curators
(art graduates, students from liberal arts departments and
their faculty, artists, critics, art historians, etc.) to curate,
and to young artists to show works, which would not be
possible to show in a commercial space.

*What is the focus of your collection? Do you concentrate on the
presentation of your collection or on organizing temporary
exhibitions?*

The focus of our collection is contemporary art from South
Asia (India, Pakistan, Bangladesh, Sri Lanka) stretching
to Central Asia and Iran. We generally organize temporary
exhibitions.

How did you choose the location of the museum and its architect?

The plot of land was bought by my husband's company.
We chose a young architect from Gujarat, who had worked
with us on another project.

*How strongly are you involved in the running of the museum
(programming, management, etc.)?*

We are completely hands on, as we have a very small team
of two or three young people. We all decide on the programming together.

Do you have an educational program?

In fact we are moving from organizing large exhibitions to
educational programs. We are creating modules for presentation in colleges. We are hoping to work with students
in realizing small exhibitions that they curate themselves.

What is your relationship with public or other institutions? Do you get (public or private) funding?

We are now starting to collaborate with other private art initiatives. Last year we collaborated with a contemporary dance residency called Gati. We paired three young artists and three young contemporary dancers. Each pair was commissioned to choreograph a piece for the premiere of the festival of contemporary dance, which was organized by Gati. We do not get any public or private funding.

In the past five years, what has been your greatest joy in running the museum? What has been the biggest challenge?

The greatest joy over the last few years has been conceiving different genres of shows with different curators. Some shows have been three years in the making. We have done shows from still/moving images to the vernacular art of India to contemporary textiles made into artworks using traditional Indian textile techniques. The greatest challenge has always been to present the shows innovatively.

What can a private museum do, that public institutions cannot? How do you respond to people who criticize the proliferation of private museums?

Private museums can take risks that public institutions cannot.

What are the greatest challenges in the long-term development of a private museum? What are your plans for the next generation?

The greatest challenges private museums face is that they are the vision of an individual or a family. Once the individual or family is no longer there—how does that vision continue?

Do you have unrealized projects?

We would like to open our collection for research. That will take a few more years to realize.

Nadia Samdani
Samdani Art Foundation, Dhaka, Bangladesh

Nadia Samdani is the cofounder and president of the Samdani Art Foundation and director of the Dhaka Art Summit. She founded the Samdani Art Foundation in 2011 together with her husband Rajeeb. Both are members of Tate Modern's International Council and founding members of Harvard University's South Asian Institute Arts Council, United States.

Year of foundation: 2011
Size: Nomadic
Number of employees: n/a
Visitors: n/a

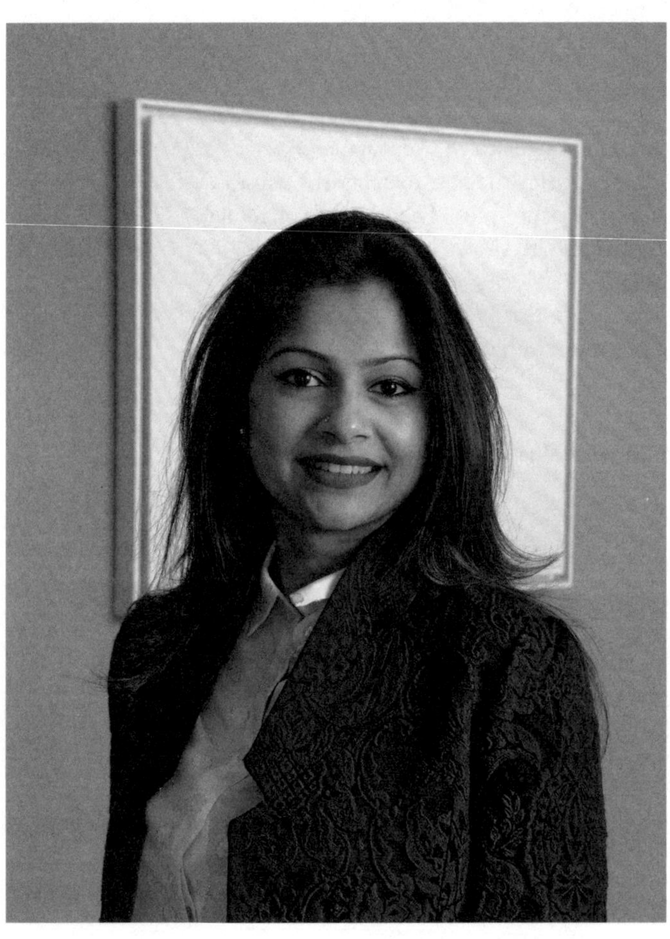

*What was your main motivation in
founding a museum?*

In Bangladesh, we do not have a
dedicated museum for contemporary art, and it is rare that an
international contemporary art
exhibition travels to the country.
We, as a country, are still somehow
disconnected from the rest of
the world with little opportunity
for the public and art students
to get involved with the progressive
thinking within the art world.
My husband Rajeeb and I wanted
to build a space for local people
to experience and learn about
contemporary art from all over the
world. This is where the idea of
creating a museum or rather in our
case, an art center, came from.
Our audience would probably never
go to a museum. In South Asia, the
term "museum" can be alienating
and considered elite, which is
why we chose the word "summit"
for the Dhaka Art Summit and "art
center" instead of museum.

With these more ambiguous terms, the audience can imagine what they want the experience to be like for them.

Did you have a specific model (i.e. an existing collection) in mind, and is there a tradition in your family of collecting art?

My father is a collector of Bangladeshi modern art and my initial collection also began with Bangladeshi modern and contemporary art, but now, as a married couple, Rajeeb and I collect art from all over the world.

We have two collections: one belongs to the Samdani Art Foundation, which is a research-based, curated collection from South Asian countries led by Diana Campbell Betancourt, Artistic Director of the Foundation. The other is our personal collection of art from all over the world; it reflects our journey as collectors. We enjoy working with Diana to join the two collections in meaningful ways— as you will see in our future space located in Sylhet in the northeast of Bangladesh. We are trying to push the local audience's idea of what art can be with it, and are therefore collecting multidisciplinary works that can transform painting into video (Shahzia Sikander's *Singing Suns*, 2016), cinema into sculpture (Anthony McCall's *Line Describing a Cone 2.0*, 1973/2010, and Lucy Raven's *Casters*, 2016), and sound into sculpture (Janet Cardiff & George Bures Miller's *Experiment in F# Minor*, 2013, and Ceal Floyer's *'Til I Get It Right*, 2005), among others. We do not like the idea of "the visual arts," and have taken a much more expanded view in building our collection.

What is the focus of your collection? Do you concentrate on the presentation of your collection or on organizing temporary exhibitions?

Our collection focuses on South Asian modern and contemporary art as well as diaspora highlights and historical influences on the region's artistic output. We collect works of the Bengal School masters and the Tagore family— who were the pioneers of modern art in greater Bengal (Bangladesh and West Bengal in India)—as well as artists who were deeply involved in the process of developing the contemporary art of South Asia. We also collect work by young and emerging South Asian artists, and have an extensive collection of international art.

We regularly lend works from our collection to museums, institutions, biennials, and exhibitions, as well as organize and produce the Dhaka Art Summit, a noncommercial research and exhibition platform for art and exchange that reexamines how we think about art and architecture from South Asia, with a focus on Bangladesh, in a regional and wider context. Currently our collection is open to the public by appointment, but with the opening of the Srihatta—Samdani Art Centre and Sculpture Park, the collection will be on view and open to the public. We have commissioned several works, including public art projects.

How did you choose the location of the museum?

Though we host the Dhaka Art Summit in the capital city Dhaka, we always wanted to set up a space in Sylhet, that would reflect the richness of the music and culture of this area. Rajeeb and I are both from Sylhet, so that was part of the pull. We are now developing our new space there on 40+ hectares of land.

Srihatta takes inspiration from Rabindranath Tagore's Shantiniketan, a University town in West Bengal, about 160 km north of Kolkata. Tagore envisioned Shantiniketan as a place of unhindered learning that would take education beyond the confines of the classroom. In this spirit, Srihatta will host arts education initiatives to connect the rural and the urban, and act as a platform for both local and international art.

How did you choose the architect?

The architect we have selected to design Srihatta is the leading Bangladeshi architect Kashef Chowdhury. In 2014, we began to include architecture in our educational initiatives, and in partnership with the Centre Pompidou, arranged a Bangladeshi architecture exhibition at the third edition of the Dhaka Art Summit in 2016. Recently, we also launched the Samdani Architecture Award for Bangladeshi architecture students.

Contemporary Bangladeshi architects are creating such innovative designs, and we wanted a Bangladeshi architect to design our space. That is how the discussion started; Kashef is the one who was able to visualize our dream. In 2016 he became the first Bangladeshi architect to participate in the Venice Architecture Biennale, exhibiting in the central pavilion, and in the same year, received the Aga Khan Award for Architecture.

How strongly are you involved in the running of the museum (programming, management, etc)?

The development of Srihatta and its future exhibitions and commissions are led by our Artistic Director and Chief Curator Diana Campbell Betancourt. We also have a wonderful team from all over the world overseeing exhibitions, development and engagement, loans, and production. Of course, we are involved when it comes to developing Srihatta, new acquisitions, and other necessary decisions, but our Artistic Director, with whom we work very closely, leads the artistic program. We strongly believe that institutions should be run by professionals; our team works independently and as a team plan and arrange our various and vast programs.

Do you have an educational program?

Education is a primary focus of the Samdani Art Foundation. We organize educational programs throughout the year. One of these initiatives is the Samdani Seminars, an informal education program we founded in 2015 to facilitate engagement between internationally renowned art professionals and local communities across Bangladesh through participatory artworks, lectures, and workshops. In 2015, the Seminars focused on exploring the possibilities of the body and the space it occupies. The premise was for artists to consider the body as the primary tool of expression, a tool that also allows the engagement with traditional arts such as painting, sculpture, and photography. The 2017 Samdani Seminars focuses on sound and listening as tools for art making. The Seminars will also consider Arte Útil, institution building, and organizational strategies for local artist-led initiatives and collectives.

For the Dhaka Art Summit 2018, we will host an Education Pavilion, which will complement the existing education infrastructure in Dhaka through free workshops, lectures, and master classes.

We have a separate fund to support Bangladeshi artists to travel to international exhibitions and residencies. As part of our education program we have supported artists to visit documenta 13, who on their return have shared their experience with local artists through seminars. For documenta 14, in addition to lending works from our collection, we are again organizing a study trip for local artists and arts professionals, this time in collaboration with the Goethe-Institut. As part of the Samdani Art Award, we are working in partnership with the Delfina Foundation to provide a residency opportunity to the winner, free of cost.

What is your relationship with public or other institutions? Do you get (public or private) funding?

We privately fund the foundation. We support several institutions and exhibitions globally, such as past exhibitions at Parasol unit in London, Kunsthalle Basel and Kunsthalle Zürich, the Shanghai Biennale, and the Venice Biennale.

We also support several other institutions, which include Tate, where Rajeeb and I are members of the International Council and their South Asian Acquisitions Committee (which Rajeeb co-chairs). We are founding members of Harvard University's South Asian Institute Arts Council. Although we do not receive any private funding, for some exhibitions we do partner with cultural institutions from around the globe such as the Bangladesh Shilpakala Academy, the Bangladesh Ministry of Cultural Affairs, the Polish Institute, Pro Helvetia-Swiss Art Council, and the Office of Contemporary Art Norway, to name but a few.

All of our events are free and open to all.

In the past five years, what has been your greatest joy in running the museum? What has been the biggest challenge?

The Samdani Art Foundation's greatest achievement has been establishing the Dhaka Art Summit. There are many international biennials in South Asia, but none of them have a regional focus, making the Summit the largest event for South Asian art in the world. It has positioned Bangladesh as a key location on the international art map. During the last edition in 2014, we welcomed 138,000 visitors over 4 days—or 3,000 people an hour. Over 800 researchers and writers from over 70 international institutions attended the Summit to extend and further their research into the region.

The Dhaka Art Summit provided a strong platform to Bangladeshi artists, with many young artists from the Samdani Art Award exhibition receiving opportunities to show their work at the Gwangju Biennale, the Shanghai Biennale, and the Colombo Biennale, curated by vienna and Kunsthalle Zürich. It is amazing to see how so many of the artists we have supported are now receiving international recognition.

For each edition of the Summit, we aim to improve our programming, which continues to be a challenge: to maintain international standards we have to train everyone from the ground up because there is still a lack of local art professionals and technical staff.

What can a private museum do, that public institutions cannot? How do you respond to people who criticize the proliferation of private museums?

Unlike public institutions, private institutions enjoy a much faster decision-making process and in the case of funding, public institutions suffer where private institutions have an edge. We can also make decisions independently from the market (we don't rely on funding from galleries) and government policies.

For example, in Bangladesh there are no other similar institutions like the one we are developing, and we can only develop it because we are privately funded. If it were a public institution, the process would have taken many years due to the funding crisis and in-fighting among the country's political groups.

The recent proliferation of private museums has had a major positive impact and made a contribution to society. We want to be unique; we are not trying to replicate the collections or models of other private institutions either within the region or elsewhere globally.

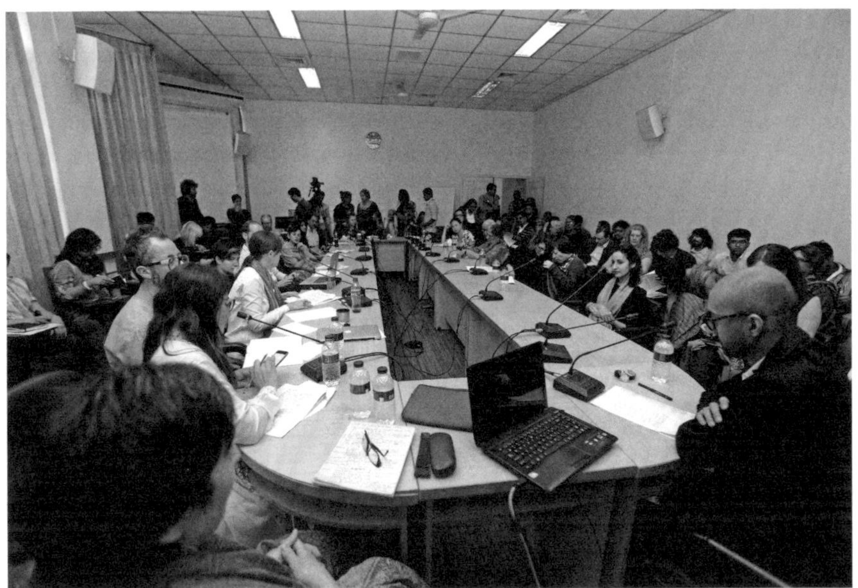

Critical Writing Ensembles, Dhaka Art Summit, 2016

What are the greatest challenges in the long-term development of a private museum? What are your plans for the next generation?

The initiative of a private museum is taken on by the patrons who nurture the institution and thus make it a success. However, the challenges come in with the next generation when they have to decide to continue the institution's legacy or leave it behind.

We are building our institution for the next generation. We have a program for school children where we arrange guided tours of the Dhaka Art Summit as well as workshops—at the Summit and through the Samdani Art Foundation—to build up their interest in art from early age. We recently hosted a Samdani Seminar with Polish artist Paweł Althamer, during which he and his "neighbors" created the communal sculpture *Rokeya*. This involved hundreds of village children from the outskirts of Sylhet in its production, with the aim of bridging understanding across social and cultural divides through the power of creativity. The interactive sculpture has already engaged hundreds of local school children and will continue to act as a space for sculpture, art workshops, and collective drawing within the belly of the sculpture.

Do you have unrealized projects?

Although we are now developing Srihatta—Samdani Art Centre and Sculpture Park in Sylhet, our dream is to build an additional space in the heart of Dhaka to display part of our permanent collection, and host exhibitions of international and Bangladeshi artists. This would be a hub for local artists to learn, share, and experience new artistic ideas. We are still looking for the right location, but we are hopeful that we will be able to fulfill this dream soon.

Patrizia Sandretto Re Rebaudengo
Fondazione Sandretto Re Rebaudengo, Turin

Patrizia Sandretto Re Rebaudengo is the founder and president of Fondazione Sandretto Re Rebaudengo established in 1995. After graduating in Economy and Business from Turin University, she started collecting contemporary art in the early 1990s.

Year of foundation: 1995
Size: 3,500 m^2
Number of employees: 15
Visitors: c. 90,000 per year

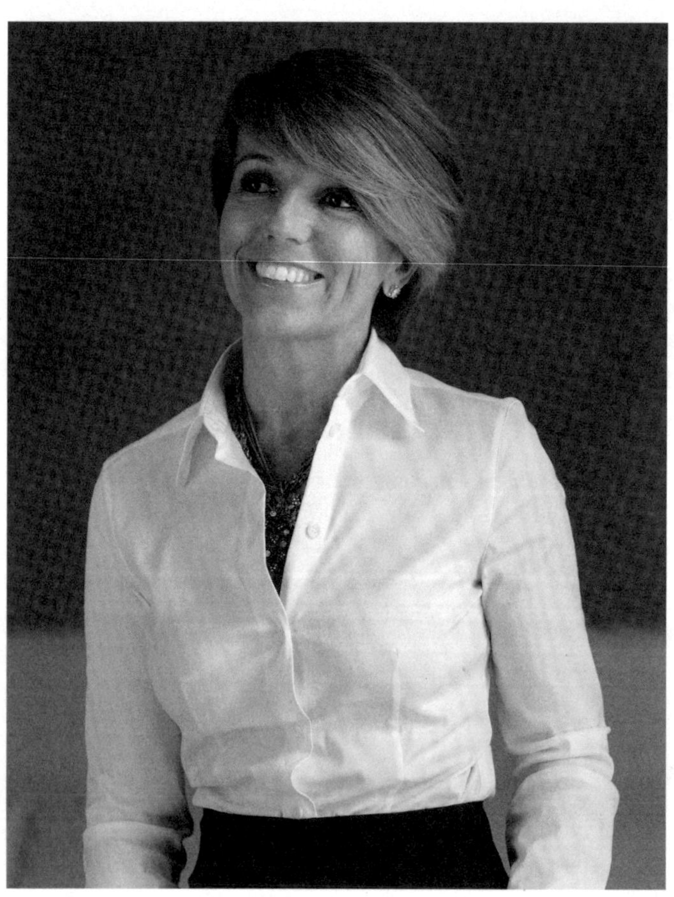

What was your main motivation in founding a museum?

Ever since I started collecting in 1992, I felt I wanted to share my works with a larger public. I have always had a desire to share my love of art, to have it as my vocation and to be more involved in the art world. My curiosity and passion led me to visit many museums and cultural institutions abroad. I remember seeing galleries and museums dedicated to Italian artists. It seemed incredible that you had to go abroad to admire Italian contemporary art. I was particularly impressed by the number of parents with small children in pushchairs that I saw visiting museums, entire families eating in museum cafeterias/restaurants. This was what inspired me to found a museum in Turin, designed for the public, and which offers a range of services to its visitors.

The lack of institutions dedicated to contemporary art in Italy at that time, the desire to support young artists and to share my collection, led me to establish the Fondazione Sandretto Re Rebaudengo in 1995. The Fondazione is a nonprofit institution, which shines a light on art and artists of today. My foundation is not purely a home for my collection, but rather a place where temporary exhibitions with the work of young and emerging artists from all over the world are shown.

Did you have a specific model (i.e. an existing collection) in mind, and is there a tradition in your family of collection art?

Art has been part of my life since I was a child; I grew up among old paintings and antiques—collecting is in my DNA. My mother used to collect antique porcelain and, as a girl, I used to collect small boxes for storing pills. Even now I don't just collect art, but also American costume jewelry. My family have always supported my enthusiasm and shared in my taste for the contemporary art I have collected.

As a collector, I was deeply inspired by exemplary women such as Peggy Guggenheim, who was always ready to help artists early on in their careers, and Gertrude Vanderbilt Whitney, who founded her own museum. I was also inspired by the history of collecting in my town, Turin. At the end of the 1960s, for example, there was a lively and important contingent of collectors, many of whom produced interesting events. I am thinking of Marcello Levi's Deposito d'Arte Presente in particular, a multidisciplinary space where large-scale works of Arte Povera were exhibited to the public.

When I opened the Fondazione I had two institutional models in mind: the German Kunsthalle and the French FRACs. The Kunsthalle is an exhibition space without a collection, it's a living laboratory where artists can experiment and produce new works. The model of the FRAC—a regional collection of contemporary art—is relevant for my activity as a private collector. My collection has no permanent home—I loan it to the Fondazione whenever required, but also to international institutions. That way, my collection is always available to the public.

*What is the focus of your collection? Do you concentrate on the
presentation of your collection or on organizing temporary exhibitions?*

To begin with, my collection followed five themes, each of
which explored aspects of artistic production from the
1980s until today: British art, artists working in Los Angeles,
Italian art, female artists, and photography. As such my
collection is more-or-less entirely contemporary. Photography is the only area of my collection that also has a historical
dimension (I have around 3,000 historical photographs
dating from the mid-1800s, which together retrace the
history of the Italian landscape).

In recent years, my interests have developed and
I can no longer categorize my collection by nationality, genre,
or medium of expression. In general though, I favor art that
has a political and social dimension, so it is this type of
work that continues to feature prominently in my collection.
Sometimes I have bought on impulse, but generally the works
have been acquired with a structured collection in mind.
For me, an interesting work of art captures the present,
anticipates the future, and, in the future, will tell a story
of the past. I try not to buy works by acclaimed artists
or by the usual "key players." I don't buy names, but works.

To begin with my collection was very "generational"—
it grew out of my friendships with artists. I was interested
in what artists of my age thought and did, as we shared
the same interests in music and literature, and watched the
same films. I was interested in the way artists from my
generation saw the world in which we were living. Through
them, I learned to look ahead, to understand art being
created by the youngest generation, and the themes and
practices that interested them.

Since I began collecting, I have always lent works to
museums and institutions. It brings me great pleasure to see
them exhibited in other spaces and to make contemporary
art accessible to more people. My collection is on permanent
loan from the Fondazione, which means that from the
outset, it has been in dialogue with other institutions and
museums, been part of exhibitions abroad, and attracted
the attention of the contemporary art world. Through
the Fondazione, the collection has been presented at
the Whitechapel Gallery in London, Kunsthalle Krems,

the Centre of Contemporary Art Znaki Czasu in Toruń
(Poland), MACRO Museum in Rome, Fundación Banco
Santander in Madrid, Sheffield Cathedral, and the Centro
de Arte Contemporáneo in Quito—to name just a few.

How did you choose the location of the museum?

Today the Fondazione has its main gallery and headquarters
in an industrial area of Turin, which was part of a major
regeneration project in the 1990s. The Fondazione has
a second venue in Guarene d'Alba, called Palazzo Re
Rebaudengo. The Palazzo is an 18th-century villa that has
been in the Re Rebaudengo family for many years. In 1997,
we converted the space in order to make it suitable for
exhibitions and opened it to the public. The Palazzo Re
Rebaudengo is also a residential space, containing eight
studios for artists and curators.

How did you choose the architect?

London-based Italian architect Claudio Silvestrin designed
the Fondazione's main space. He was the winner of an
international competition launched in 1998, for which more
than 30 architectural firms across Europe applied. A jury
comprised of Francesco Bonami, Hans Ulrich Obrist, Marco
Folin, and myself then chose our favorite. The applications
were anonymous—we chose Silvestrin based purely on
the strength of his application.

    The building is a simple, light, minimalist structure,
a contemporary container for a new generation of artists.
The museum has a 1,500 square meter exhibition space,
a project room for video installations, and an educational
department. It also has a 144-seat auditorium, equipped with
the latest audio/visual technology, a bookshop, a cafeteria
especially designed by the artist Rudolf Stingel, as well as
a restaurant on the first floor. The building is ideally suited
to its purpose, from the installation of artworks to the ease
of access for the public.

    The internal structure was designed to be a neutral
space where artists could work freely, without any visual
conflict or distraction caused by the surrounding architecture.
It was also designed to be highly versatile, allowing for the

creation and installation of large-scale works. The materials themselves further underline the minimalistic nature of the architecture, from the Lecce stone used for the external structure to the cedarwood used for the furniture contained.

How strongly are you involved in the running of the museum (programming, management, etc.)?

I am deeply involved in the running of Fondazione Sandretto Re Rebaudengo—it's a full-time job and my main occupation. I work side-by-side with my staff, helping to develop our exhibition program, and planning our collateral events. I also travel a lot, not only to see exhibitions, fairs, biennials, and to visit artists' studios, but also because I am a member of a number of different international councils of museums such as Tate Gallery and the Serpentine Galleries in London, the Philadelphia Museum of Art, and the New Museum and the Museum of Modern Art in New York.

Do you have an educational program?

The Fondazione has an Education and Art Mediation Department. Art mediation is very important to us. Our cultural mediators establish and encourage direct contact between visitors and the exhibitions, planting ideas, stimulating debate and discussing individual interpretations, all while standing in front of the art itself.

To be able to do this, our mediators (graduates in fine art or history of art) follow a training program especially designed and implemented by the Fondazione consisting of lectures and workshops about theories and methodologies related to the field. Instead of the traditional guided tour, we favour a more informal and conversational approach, where we provide information and suggestions to encourage dialogue and give visitors the opportunity to offer their own readings of the works.

The art mediation service is available during the Fondazione's opening hours, in English and Italian. It is free and no reservation is required. We believe it promotes a drop-in mentality, and gives the sense that we are an open-minded museum that welcomes people of all backgrounds and offers everyone learning opportunities.

We firmly believe in the idea of an accessible museum that enables each visitor to take advantage of the cultural content we offer. This is the reason why we have so many different projects, involving many different groups of people. This includes special education programs for migrants (children, teenagers, and adults), family Sundays every month, Big Draw! events (the campaign for drawing) twice a year, free workshops for adults on Thursday evenings, intensive workshops for teenagers and university students, special projects for infant and primary schools throughout the academic year, activities for those with special needs (working closely with the Italian Union of Blind People), and e-learning initiatives.

Another thing we do is to regularly evaluate the cultural impact of our projects. The purpose of this is to show that they have concrete results, and also to improve the quality of the programmes. These are then kept for internal use and shared with our stakeholders.

We believe that understanding the arts is a vital component in everyone's education and development. Contemporary art often uses unconventional methods, media, and messages to push the boundaries of traditional art forms, and we want to challenge people; to discover how important it is to welcome those forms of thinking and creating in their lives.

In addition to education, the Fondazione gives great importance to Lifelong Learning, through an intense programme of workshops conceived and led by the mediators, in collaboration with artists or professionals from different fields, and dedicated to adults. We feel that specialized training is crucial. Since 2007, the Young Curators Residency Program has given three curators from the most important schools in the world the chance to discover Italian contemporary art, through trips and studio visits. They are then provided with a space in the Fondazione where they can stage an exhibition to culminate their research. In 2012, the Fondazione also launched Campo, an independent study program for Italian curators, which consists of lessons and field trips in Italy and the rest of Europe.

What is your relationship with public or other institutions? Do you get (public or private) funding?

I think public and private institutions need to start a new
era of collaboration with each other. Private institutions
play a public role in offering a community service through
their exhibitions, educational departments, activities, etc.,
and the aim of both private and public institutions is to
promote contemporary art and support artists. As such
I strongly believe that public and private institutions should
work side-by-side to reach these goals.

In 2014, my foundation promoted the creation of a
network of private foundations for contemporary art in Italy,
all of which have a public program of exhibitions and have
been known to support and promote artists. The Comitato
Fondazioni Italiane Arte Contemporanea unites 14 foundations along the peninsula—from Turin to Venice, and Milan
to Catania—with the aim of strengthening our cooperation
so we can better promote contemporary art in Italy.
These foundations own private collections, that—grouped
together—form the largest contemporary art collection
in Italy.

The Comitato are also collaborating with various
public institutions, in particular the Minister of Cultural
Heritage and Activities and Tourism (MiBACT), to promote
a new and more intense cooperation between national
institutions and private foundations, with the aim of promoting Italian contemporary artists and working on education
projects that will bring a contemporary art to an even wider
public, together. I think that this first step demonstrates
that there is willingness among public institutions to
cooperate, but also to recognize private foundations as a
qualified interlocutor in the Italian contemporary art scene.

*In the past five years, what has been your greatest joy in running
the museum? What has been the biggest challenge?*

I am greatly delighted by everyday life at the Fondazione:
small children visiting our exhibitions, a visitor immersed in
a conversation with a cultural mediator in front of an artwork,
disabled people who have access to the exhibitions thanks
to mediators who are specifically trained to help them.

Many joys come from the artists, from their research
and their successes. Ian Cheng, for example, to whom
the Fondazione devoted a solo show in 2015, produced

the first video of his trilogy *Emissaries* at the Fondazione,
which has since been displayed at Migros Museum für
Gegenwartskunst in 2016 and MoMA PS1 in 2017.

One of the greatest challenges was presenting Adrián
Villar Rojas' solo exhibition, *Rinascimento*, at the Fondazione
in 2015. The Fondazione was completely transformed by
Adrian's project, which involved bringing in humungous
stones from Turkey especially for it. The exhibition brought
the Fondazione back to its origins. It was a daring project,
carried out with great passion.

What can a private museum do, that public institutions cannot?
How do you respond to people who criticize the proliferation of
private museums?

A private museum is first of all an independent structure.
This means that it can be more flexible and consequently
more able to experiment with new approaches and projects.
For example, in 2002, Fondazione Sandretto Re Rebaudengo
introduced cultural mediation, a service that was only recently
adopted by public museums in Italy. I am also thinking about
our residency and curatorial programs, which are training
and educational opportunities for professional figures, that
the Italian academic world is unable to acknowledge.

Over the last 20 years in Italy, private museums,
and more specifically, private foundations, have played
a key role in compensating for the public institutions' lack
of commitment to contemporary art (for example, the first
national museum for contemporary art, the MAXXI, was
opened in 2010 in Rome). This is the context in which
the proliferation of private museums should be understood.

Private museums are not static structures, they are
not just spaces devoted to the conservation and exhibition
of a collection, but they can be cultural centers that, together
with the public, actively contribute to the production of
contemporary culture.

What are the greatest challenges in the long-term development of
a private museum? What are your plans for the next generation?

The challenge for an institution like mine is to maintain its
innovative and experimental character, to fuel the spirit of

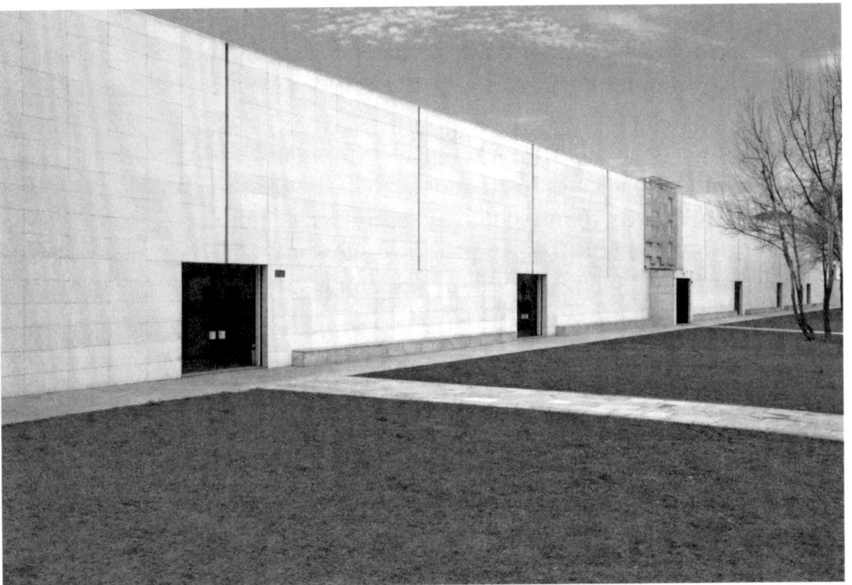

Fondazione Sandretto Re Rebaudengo, Turin

research that distinguishes the Fondazione. This also
means that through our activities we have to keep on finding,
supporting, and promoting the newest generations of
artists, curators, and professionals.

We also face funding issues, especially in a period like
this when both public and private resources have shrunk.
In this area too we try to find different solutions, looking for
new, unusual partnerships, and pointing to the Fondazione
as a philanthropic model supporting contemporary culture.

*In September 2017, you announced the opening of a new venue of
the Fondazione Sandretto in Madrid. What are your motivations
in opening a venue outside your own country and what are your
expectations?*

Fundación Sandretto Re Rebaudengo Madrid was established
in January 2017. In September 2015, having visited the
Matadero area, I contacted the City of Madrid, applying
for the concession and the internal renewal of the Nave 9,
with the aim of developing the Fondazione's activities
through the support of young artists, the permanent display
of the collection, and the realization of educational projects.
After several months developing the project with the City,
we finally received a state concession for a 50-year period.
On January 10, 2017, Fundación Sandretto Re Rebaudengo
Madrid was officially set up. The Fundación venue will open
in 2019.

I had been thinking of extending our horizons for
a long time, considering the possibility of setting up a new
project outside Turin. I evaluated various possibilities and
different locations, both in Italy and abroad. The choice
of Madrid lies first of all in my love for Spain that I consider
my second homeland. I spent some time in Spain as a
young girl. I have many friends there. I'm fascinated with
Spanish culture and I get on well with Spanish people.
Besides that there are many other reasons to choose Madrid:
it's a great global capital and a bridge to Latin America—
a continent that today plays a leading role on the contemporary art scene. Moreover, I have been invited to show
part of my collection in Spain a few times, and I have always
had a good feedback. I literally fell in love at first sight
with Matadero. This international Centre for contemporary

creation supported by the Government's Department of
Arts, Sports, and Tourism of Madrid City Council impressed
me. I was intrigued by its architecture, its typical red bricks
facades, and its transformation from a early 20th-century
slaughterhouse to a vibrant interdisciplinary center for
contemporary culture. As in Turin, I was interested in the life
of a district which was not that of a typical tourist visit, and
in the impacts that artistic and cultural activities may have on
a social fabric.

The Fundación will primarily be an exhibition center,
focusing on research and the production of new shows and
works. In keeping with our philosophy, it will contain spaces
for an educational department, for cultural mediation and
specialized training, for artists and curators residencies.
To design the interiors I chose architect David Adjaye who
works in collaboration with Spanish architect Arturo Franco.
I asked them to work on the idea of a welcoming place,
designed for works and artists, but also for the visiting public,
and the schools and families involved in our laboratories.
As in our two other venues, the principle of accessibility will
be applied by removing both physical and cultural barriers.

In the artistic and cultural project for the Fundación
Sandretto Re Rebaudengo Madrid, a leading role is played
by the collection. A selection of 100 works has been given on
a long-term loan to the Fundación and the Nave 9 will
present the works on a rotating basis. The Fundación's
activities and exhibition program will pay a special attention
to the Spanish and Latin American artistic scenes and
we will look at the local curators, educators, art mediators,
and art professionals too, so we plan to involve a local staff
for managing our activities in Madrid together with my
closest collaborators from Turin.

Do you have unrealized projects?

Conceiving projects is part of my daily life: every day I work
with unrealized projects—beginning with an idea, and seeking
to make it a reality. Sometimes it takes years. At the moment,
I am particularly interested in designing new spaces, new
exhibitions, and developing a relationship with a larger public,
one that is more and more involved in contemporary art.

Mario Saradar
Saradar Collection, Beirut

Mario Saradar is Chairman-CEO of Marius Saradar Holding (MSH), and serves as the
Chairman-CEO of Saradar Bank. He has been involved in the cultural scene in Lebanon for
many years. The creation of the Saradar Collection is the outcome of his desire to ensure
a legacy of Lebanese art.

Year of foundation: 2012
Size: n/a
Number of employees: 2
Visitors: n/a

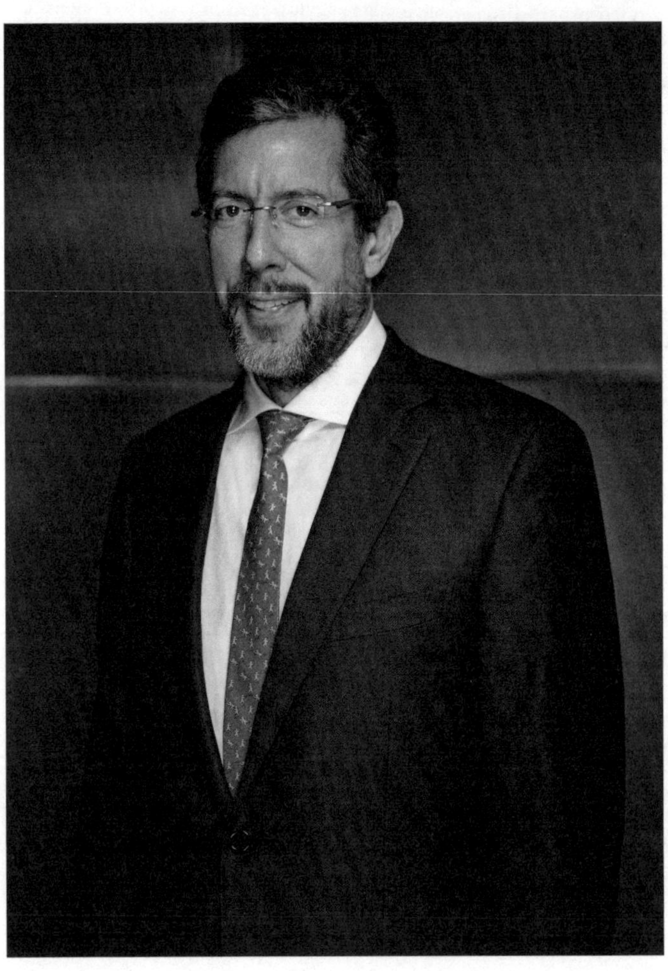

Saradar is a private collection, but not a museum. Instead it is going public online and with programs in 2018. What are the reasons for that and for not founding a museum?

Saradar Collection was launched in 2012. It is an initiative built around a private collection with a public mission to preserve, study, and share modern and contemporary art from Lebanon. It grew out of a desire to address the lack of institutional collections in the country and to build a local collection to share with the public. Considering the growing international interest in art from Lebanon, we intended to not only support artists, but also ensure that a significant part of the country's artistic heritage is preserved and shared.

In answer to why the Saradar Collection didn't consider establishing a museum: though museums are the natural place for sharing, exhibiting, studying, and documenting artworks, one should bear in mind that museums also have limits and constraints in terms of management and programing. They often suffer from a lack of flexibility. Nowadays, dynamic change and adaptation are key, and this applies also to the cultural environment. At the local level, the artistic scene is constantly evolving as many new projects are announced. It is in this context that for small initiatives flexibility becomes a must to adapt strategies to new cultural environments. In our case, our first concern remains the collection and how to find the best approach to build knowledge about our collection and share it, both inside and outside our country. In order to achieve our goal, we have been developing a series of programs taking the collection as a starting point in order to create knowledge, encourage critical thinking, experiment with new forms of curatorial discourse, explore other ways of exhibiting artworks, and finally challenge the traditional ways of showing artworks, and liberate them from the natural limits of a museum. A museum is definitely not the right answer for our project. Nevertheless, we still believe that artworks must be physically accessible, and as such we are currently working on a project to achieve this through "open storage."

What shape did the initiative have in the past and what are the plans for the future?

Since its inception, the Saradar Collection has evolved at its own pace, but always remains attentive to the local artistic scene as well as to its needs and lacks.

As a first step, we have been concentrating our efforts on the first acquisitions. Taking into consideration the level of responsibility entailed, and considering the lack of institutional cultural projects on the local scene, we decided to form a consulting committee composed of local and international experts to assist us in building the collection. The committee defines the curatorial framework of the collection, recommends artworks, orients acquisitions, and thus allows us to make better and more enlightened choices. To date the collection includes more than 40 artists and has assembled 250 artworks. In parallel to the acquisitions we have been developing many programs around the collection in order to enrich its database, encourage critical

thinking, and produce knowledge around it. This is where
we stand today: in the middle of an interim period prior
to going onto the public stage.

We will be moving toward the second phase of the
project very soon as the Saradar Collection will be accessible
online with links and related documents through its website
in spring 2018, after which the public programs will start
in fall 2018.

*Did you have a specific model (i.e. an existing collection) in mind,
and is there a tradition in your family of collecting art?*

Family members are individual collectors. There is no collecting tradition per se, but individual interest in the arts in
general. It should be noted that the Saradar Collection is completely distinct from any family member's private collection.

The Saradar Collection aims to answer the local
cultural artistic context needs. Our initiative is not inspired
by a specific model, but rather our aim is to combine
practices from different initiatives.

What is the focus of your collection?

Artworks are primarily by Lebanese artists from modern
and contemporary periods, but the collection also includes
regional and international artists with ties to Lebanon.
The collection contains a range of mediums such as works
on paper, painting, photography, video, installation, and
sculpture.

*How strongly are you involved in the running of the initiative
(programming, management, etc.)?*

From the beginning I decided to keep a distance between
the project and myself. I carefully follow the growth of
our collection and oversee the way our mission is being
accomplished.

Do you have an educational program?

We will launch educational programs simultaneously with
our public programs. Meanwhile the Saradar Collection has

been developing the program "Introducing Art," dedicated to colleagues, which aims to encourage appreciation and knowledge of art.

What is your relationship with public or other institutions? Do you get (public or private) funding?

The Saradar Collection is financially backed exclusively by the Saradar family. As part of the mission to share the collection with the local and international public, the Saradar Collection offers work on loan for museums and other exhibitions spaces in and outside Lebanon. Moreover, through the programing of further collaborations with other institutions, the Saradar Collection intends to develop art spaces, both locally and internationally. This approach will definitely help us in further promoting ourselves through the creation of exchange platforms.

In the past five years, what has been your greatest joy in running the initiative? What has been the biggest challenge?

The past five years have been very challenging as this was the launching phase. I have to say that it was very exciting to follow the growth of our collection and progressively prepare its visibility. The major challenge we constantly face is the dynamic changes in our local cultural scene, and the unstable political climate and adverse economic situation in Lebanon.

What can a private initiative or museum do, that a public institution cannot? How do you respond to people who criticize the proliferation of private museums?

In terms of the Lebanese art scene, one could say that the proliferation of private initiatives can enrich the cultural landscape, which is currently suffering from a real lack in public institutions. Public funds allocated to culture are extremely low; most cultural projects in Lebanon are supported by private funds.

However, in the absence of cultural public policy, the action led by each of the initiatives should be conducted with professionalism and in an ethical manner in order to build a cultural landscape that will benefit the local population.

Private initiatives are without any doubt very important as they help to promote cultural projects through dedicated funds. Unfortunately, the projects are often very "owner centric," and remain attached to the individual who initiated them, as opposed to public institutions that are organized in a more decentralized manner.

What are the greatest challenges in the long-term development of a private engagement that goes public? What are your plans for the next generation?

Private structures face major issues regarding sustainability: cultural institutions become a landmark and a reference only after the "test of time." Through the Saradar Collection we intend to ensure a legacy of art in Lebanon.

Do you have unrealized projects?

Of course I have, I always do. First I need to initiate them and put them on the right track before sharing them.

Bernar Venet
Venet Foundation, Le Muy

Bernar Venet is a sculptor living in Paris, the South of France, and New York where he moved in 1967. He has been exhibited widely in museum and gallery exhibitions in Europe, the United States, and Asia for the last 40 years.

Year of foundation: 2014
Size: 2,715 m² (includes gallery, exhibition space in factory, Chapel)
Number of employees: n/a
Visitors: n/a

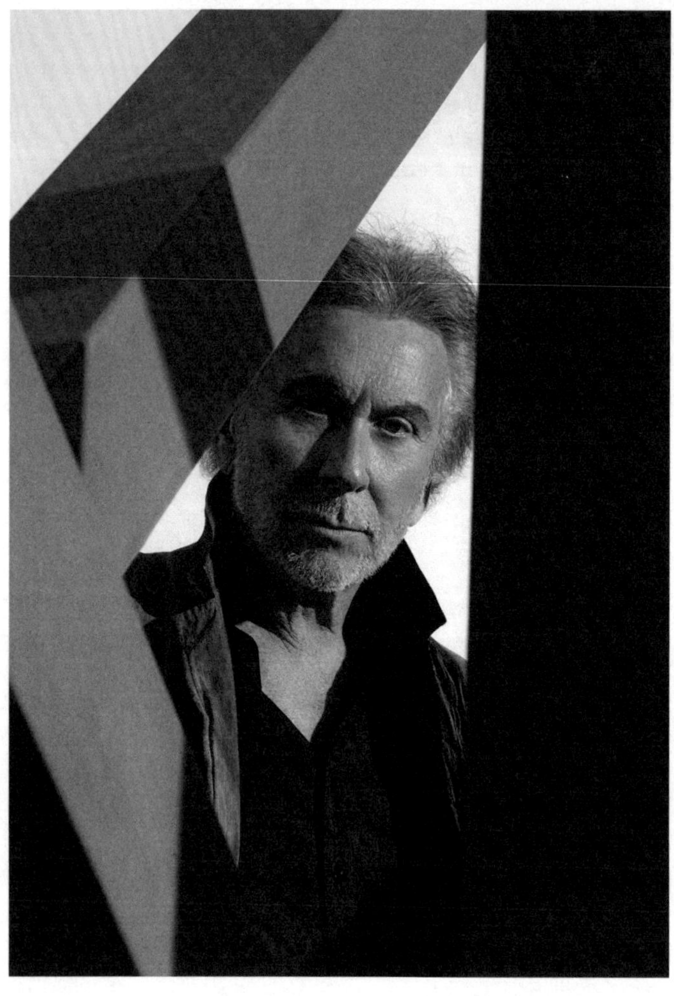

What was your main motivation in founding a museum?

When we realized that an audience well versed in contemporary art was showing interest in visiting the site and the collection, my family and I thought it would be better if we created a foundation to ensure the long-term viability of this unique group of artworks. I've been handed the chance above all to give back to society what society allowed me to acquire throughout a very privileged life.

Did you have a specific model in mind, and is there a tradition in your family of collecting art?

The word "art" was never a part of my family's vocabulary. During my childhood, culture was a luxury that was a far cry from our primary concerns about staying alive. The place where I was born, a small village in the French Alps, was far from museums and art centers, and didn't foster a potential commitment to the artistic avant-garde. Because of the particular circumstances surrounding the death of my father, I discovered for the first time in Grenoble what a museum was, and better still in light of my future career, what a *contemporary* art museum was. Arriving in New York in 1966, I immediately found myself smack in the middle of the avant-garde of the time. And when Donald Judd acquired Marfa, he showed me the slides and told me about his project, which was to show his works and those of several others in the best possible conditions. Discovering the Chinati Foundation was a revelation that gave me the energy and ambition to develop my own property at Le Muy and make it into a foundation.

What is the focus of your collection? Do you concentrate on the presentation of your collection or on organizing temporary exhibitions?

My wife Diane and I mostly collect artists of my generation. Which means the sculptors mainly connected with minimal art with whom I was spending time when I arrived in New York in 1966—Donald Judd, Sol LeWitt, Carl Andre, Dan Flavin, Robert Morris … artists whose spare aesthetic and theoretical investigations are akin to my personal art making. Often those works were the result of friendly exchanges. Later I was able to acquire at very favorable terms (because the art market was more reasonable then than it is now) works by other friends like Robert Motherwell, Ellsworth Kelly, and Frank Stella … Today the foundation is home to the collection, which is mainly exhibited in a very old building that has been beautifully renovated, and we also have a sculpture park for works that can be shown outdoors, pieces by Richard Long, Larry Bell, Arman, Anthony Caro, Phillip King, among others. All of these works are part of the permanent collection, but each year we also inaugurate a solo show in one of the buildings during the summer months. After Jean Tinguely and James Turrell in the last two years, we are now going to feature the work of Fred Sandback.

How did you choose the location of the museum?

I was born in Provence and lived for a few years in Nice.
So it was to that region that I wanted to return and create
this foundation, too. Le Muy is a privileged spot, and its
location just a few minutes away from a highway exit in the
south of France makes it an ideal stopping-off point. I was
lucky to find this exceptional site, which has extraordinary
potential for development.

How did you choose the architect?

The site already boasted an old mill from the 16th century
and a large, though abandoned, factory. Initially work was
done to allow us to live and install works of art there. It was
only after about 15 years of inhabiting the property that we
had the idea of constructing a new gallery that would be
able to house temporary exhibitions. We turned to Charles
Berthier, a young and unknown architect who was very
creative and had just graduated from architecture school.
A mutual acquaintance recommended him.

*How much are you involved in the running of the museum
(programing, management, etc.)?*

This is about my legacy, so I'm naturally inclined to get
involved daily, initiate work, and oversee it. Decisions are
made in agreement with the director of the Foundation.
Those decisions mainly concern the selection of the artist
who is exhibited each summer and the works that are going
to be shown.

Do you have an educational program?

Many school and children's groups come to visit the summer
exhibitions at the foundation. We support art school students
by awarding a prize each year jointly with the City of Nice.
We host researchers and historians, and are planning
to open a library that students will be welcome to use.

*What is your relationship with public or other institutions? Do you get
(private or public) funding?*

To date we have had no public financing. I have assumed
all costs on my own. So we have had to answer to no one.
One day we will have to think about that to ensure the
Foundation's viability in the long term. We are creating
a "Friends of the Venet Foundation Association" to be able
to receive dues and gifts. The Association will also receive
profits from the sale of tie-in products. We are in contact
with other institutions to arrange loans of artworks.
The whole collection has been the subject of two exhibitions
in the past, at the Espace de l'Art Concret in Mouans-
Sartoux, and at the Musée des Abattoirs in Toulouse.

*In the past five years what has been your greatest joy in running
the museum? What has been the biggest challenge?*

Our greatest satisfaction comes from the ability to acquire
major artworks by important artists. Our sculpture park
is becoming exceptionally important; two years ago it didn't
even exist in our minds.

*What can a private museum do, that public institutions cannot?
How do you respond to the people who criticize the proliferation
of private museums?*

Our constraints are different. One of the main differences
is that we are not obliged to "get results" in terms of turning
a profit. We do draw fewer visitors of course, but everyone
who comes is entitled to a guided tour. We offer the general
public the conditions of a private tour. Moreover, our choice
of exhibitions only depends on the quality we see in them
and our desire to display that quality, not on the sale of
tickets. This allows us to show demanding artists. Our
attachment to minimalism has found favor with critics and
our audience, yet that direction would be difficult to maintain
for a museum that was dependent on receipts from ticket
sales. It's true that nowadays there is a proliferation of
private museums, and we can only wonder what will happen
to them in 50 years time. I find that all the more surprising
inasmuch as when I began my career as an artist there was

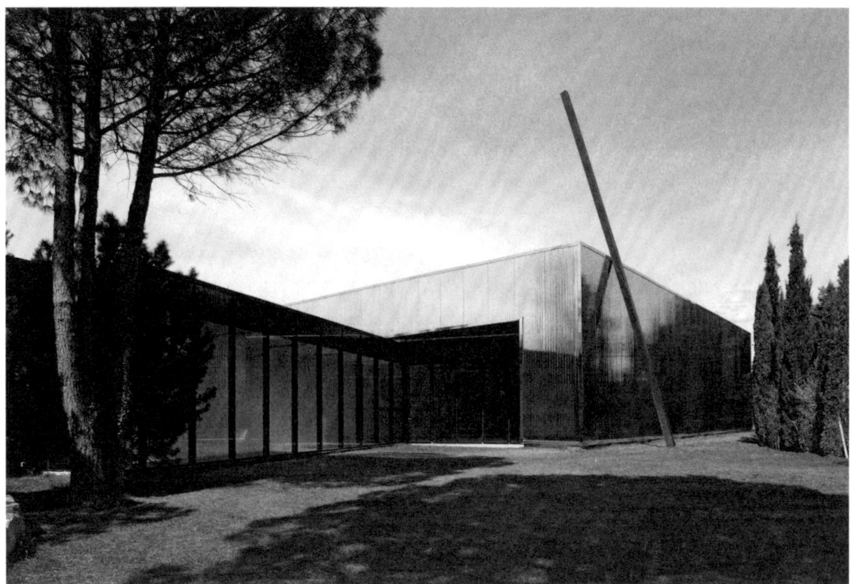

View of the new gallery with Bernar Venet's *Diagonal of 74.3°*, 2006
Painted steel, height: 15 meters

practically no venue for showing the art we were producing. The development of what is available culturally can only benefit the public and artists. It is to that development that we owe the growing interest in contemporary art, and I'm delighted. There is a real audience of enthusiasts that goes beyond the circle of professionals.

What are the greatest challenges in the long-term development of a private museum? What are your plans for the next generation?

Financing is certainly the greatest challenge. Especially when, like me, you aren't a millionaire and you sacrifice the greater part by far of your income to improving it and keeping it alive. I foresee giving up works that we'll be able to sell to guarantee the Foundation's current operating standards, and the Board is working on diversifying the sources of financing. The next generation will have serious challenges to meet, including a bigger opening in the spring and summer, a second annual exhibition, and preserving the originality of the Foundation while following new artists.

Do you have unrealized projects?

Lots … but not for long! First, there are the artworks I dream of acquiring—hoping that the chance comes up. There is the construction of a library, to make the archives available to students and researchers. I'd like to see a restaurant open to increase the sociability of the place, so that visitors who come to see us, sometimes from so far away, can prolong their visit. And if only we could build one or two exhibition venues, I could show more of my work as well as pieces from the collection that we keep in storage.

Lu Xun
Sifang Art Museum, Nanjing

Lu Xun is an art collector and founder and director of the Sifang Art Museum. He and his father Lu Jun initiated the development of an art and architecture complex in Nanjing.

Year of foundation: 2013
Size: 3,300 m^2
Number of employees: 15
Visitors: 80,000

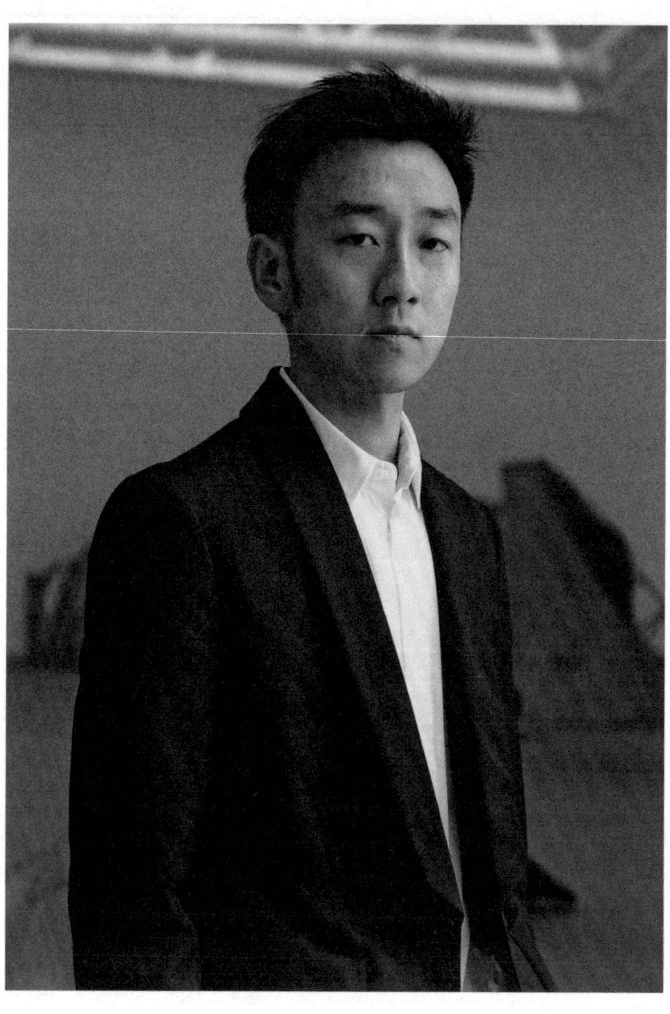

What was your main motivation in founding a museum?

The mission is to make the best of contemporary art and architecture available to a broad public by providing a unique experience.

Did you have a specific model (i.e. an existing collection) in mind, and is there a tradition in your family of collecting art?

The tradition of collecting is strong as my family is the biggest collector of archival documents and manuscripts from the Chiang Kai-shek era, covering all aspects of the history of that period [around 1911–1946]. My contemporary art collection is less comprehensive and not historical, but is very rooted in current points of interests and very much about the relations between individual artworks and artists in a given context.

What is the focus of your collection? Do you concentrate on the presentation of your collection or on organizing temporary exhibitions?

The collection is about art that is relevant for our time and it has three main parts: permanent architectural commissions, permanent art commissions, and several hundred artworks that range from large installations to performative pieces that are totally immaterial.

Both the presentation of the collection and temporary exhibitions are traditionally important aspects of museum activity. Collection shows take place every two years, and our temporary exhibitions are not necessarily temporary, but long-term, as we initiate yearly research-based projects and many permanent commissions.

How did you choose the location of the museum?

The location is a lush, naturally forested area outside the main city of Nanjing. I wanted to give visitors a sense of retreat rather than going to a museum building. The idea is a holistic experience of enjoying nature, architecture, and art, while having the amenities of nice restaurants and spas.

How did you choose the architect?

The selection process was a collaborative project with Japanese architect Arata Isozaki and Chinese architect Liu Jiakun.

How strongly are you involved in the running of the museum (programming, management, etc.)?

Very strongly.

Do you have an educational program?

Yes. Our educational program is not only for art audiences, but also for young artists and curators. We regularly hold workshops, lectures, etc., for them.

*What is your relationship with public or other institutions? Do you get
(public or private) funding?*

Most of our funding comes from the mother company Sifang
Corporation. For specific initiatives we get a small percent-
age of funding from government and private sponsors.

*In the past five years, what has been your greatest joy in running
the museum? What has been the biggest challenge?*

The greatest joy has always come from times when I feel I
have made a difference, either for the audience or for artists
and other art world professionals. The greatest challenge
has always been keeping at it. It's a long road for both a
collection and for an institution to establish its reputation.

*What can a private museum do, that public institutions cannot?
How do you respond to people who criticize the proliferation of
private museums?*

Private initiatives are sometimes more flexible, forward
thinking, and interesting compared to their public counterparts, just like the comparison between start-ups and big
corporations in the commercial world. I actually don't know
what the criticism is for private museums, isn't it a case of
the more the merrier? I'd like to think that way. In the
future, some of them will close, some of them will merge
and restructure like everything in the history books. Good
things will remain.

*What are the greatest challenges in the long-term development of
a private museum? What are your plans for the next generation?*

Building audience, identifying good artists and projects,
achieving sustainability are all still valid, but I think the
most important challenge is that as private initiatives,
we need to always stay at the forefront, and move forward
together with the greatest artists, architects, and thinkers
of our time, while keeping our mission the same.

Do you have unrealized projects?

The most important "unrealized" project is a pavilion
designed by Japanese architect SANAA. The design is ten
years old, but Chinese building capability had to catch
up with the level of sophistication they require. However,
we are completing the building this year, with many of
the problems solved by a new wave of building technologies
in China today.

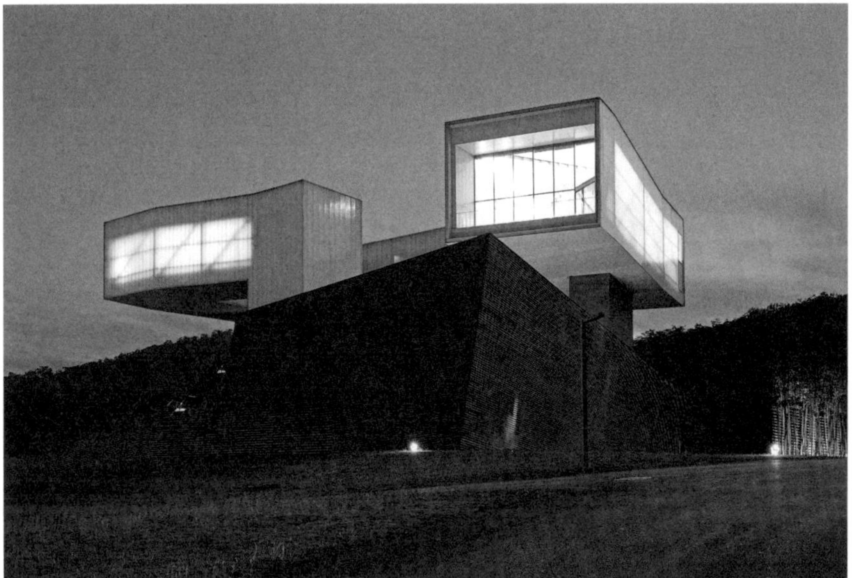

Sifang Art Museum, Nanjing

Anita Zabludowicz
Zabludowicz Collection, London, Sarvisalo, and New York

Anita Zabludowicz trained as an interior designer. She began collecting art in the 1990s and together with her husband Poju, the chief executive of the equity firm Tamares, she collects contemporary art with a focus on Conceptual art, film, and digital works.

Year of foundation: 1994 (collection); 2007 (exhibition space, London); 2010 (temporary project space, New York) and different display spaces in Sarvisalo for Residency Program activities
Size: 748 m^2 (exhibition space, London)
Number of employees: 13
Visitors: c. 120,000 per year

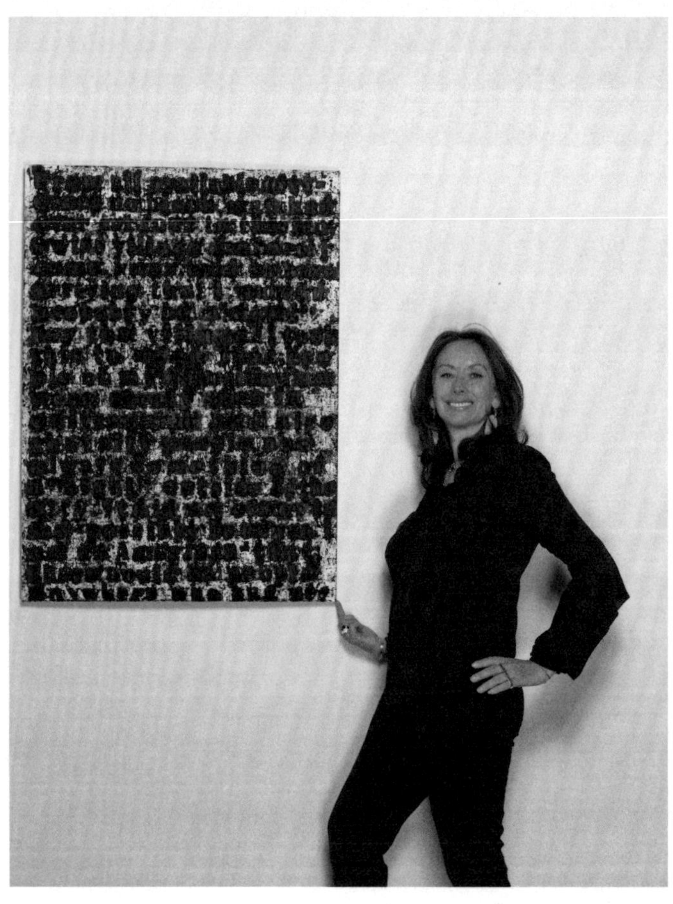

What was your main motivation in founding a museum?

Since we started collecting in the mid-1990s it became increasingly apparent to us that the younger more experimental artists we were collecting were not receiving the kind of institutional support that they needed to push their practice further. By the mid-2000s we had a substantial collection of art, bigger than we could show in our home, and mostly by early career artists. Rather than let this sit in crates in warehouses, it was important that this work be seen; we wanted to support those artists expand their practice and produce ambitious new work. We decided we needed a space in 2004 and finally opened in 2007. This move certainly changed the focus of all our activities. I would not say we are a private museum—rather a privately funded, publically-minded exhibition space and a private collection of artworks—but I do like the idea of being one in the future. Perhaps that is where we are headed as our organization matures alongside the works we collect and the artists we work with.

Did you have a specific model (i.e. an existing collection) in mind, and is there a tradition in your family of collecting art?

My husband and I are the first collectors in either of our families and we have learnt a lot since we started. We have had some very good guidance from artists, galleries, and museums along the way. But the collection is very personal and has grown organically over the last 20 or so years. We don't work with advisers, but with our curatorial team, we look for work that we are passionate about. There were and are many inspirational precursors to us—the Rubell Family Collection in Miami and the Kramlich Collection in San Francisco are often on our minds.

What is the focus of your collection? Do you concentrate on the presentation of your collection or on organizing temporary exhibitions?

Our collection is focused on emerging art, but after more than 20 years many of those artists are now well into maturity. We started collecting artists at an early point in their careers because it felt the most natural and accessible. This has continued to be our focus with subsequent generations of artists although we still support many of those we collected from the start. With our program we try to reflect both of these aspects. We have three major temporary exhibitions a year, one in which we curate works from the collection bringing together works by different generations in thematic group shows. Our fall exhibition is always a new commission in which we support an early-career artist to produce an ambitious new body of work for the space. And for our third show we mentor curating students from different London-based universities to curate a show from the collection. Alongside this we also run a small project space on site in which we do shorter exhibitions with UK-based artists who don't as yet have commercial representation, giving practices that are sometimes less market-friendly a valuable platform to make new work.

How did you choose the location of the museum?

We started looking for a building in 2005 and found this beautiful Victorian Methodist Chapel on the "at risk" register. It is a Grade II* listed building that the Council wanted to preserve for public use.[1] It's located not far from our home in North London, in an area that is not an existing art hub—we wanted to break some new ground. We are a hidden gem for many visitors, and even though a few other spaces have opened near us now, we pride ourselves on ensuring our visitors always have a great experience.

How did you choose the architect?

We worked with Allford Hall Monaghan Morris who had a lot of experience of repurposing existing buildings and had recently finished the Tea Building in Shoreditch. We wanted a very light-touch renovation to the building so that we stayed raw and true to the original fabric of the space. We wanted a building artists would feel free to work in, rather than a pristine white cube, and the architects worked with that. We have one of the most distinctive art spaces in London. The architecture has become a really important part of every exhibition we put on, and offers artists and our team an interesting set of challenges and restrictions to work with.

How strongly are you involved in the running of the museum (programming, management, etc.)?

I'm not a curator, and from the outset I was very clear that the program should be run by a team who have that specialized knowledge and skills. But I am very passionate about what we do and will offer my advice and insight on the works in the collection to the team as they are developing the program. I meet with the team as often as I can to share with them new artists that I have encountered and works that I have seen. We pool our research and knowledge. But I let them get on with it.

Do you have an educational program?

Education has been an integral part of our program from the very start. In fact we think of everything we do from an educational perspective in terms of professional development for the artists and curators we work with. In terms of our audiences we very actively work with universities, especially in our Testing Ground project where they curate one of our three major annual shows. During Testing Ground we also run a week-long creative and professional workshop called Master Class, in which artists from all over the country are mentored by leading international artists. To accompany each of our exhibitions, we run weekly family art workshops to allow young children to creatively explore the themes of a show, and we also run a full program of talks and live events for adult audiences. It's totally natural for us to do this and has been right from the beginning.

What is your relationship with public or other institutions? Do you get (public or private) funding?

We are very fortunate at the moment to be able to fund all of our activities ourselves. My husband and I have always been active in philanthropic giving, and continue to donate to other public institutions in a variety of ways. Our collection is always open to other institutions for loans, and over the years a number of exhibitions we have curated have gone on to tour to museums in spaces around the United Kingdom and internationally. We do not seek any public funds for our activities.

In the past five years, what has been your greatest joy in running the museum? What has been the biggest challenge?

We have reached a certain level of maturity in the past five years and that is a real joy—seeing things work well, and the artists getting recognition they deserve for the incredible hard work they put in. The greatest challenge is our ambition, we want to constantly keep moving forward, this is what keeps us alive, and it comes from the artists. We are a very artist-centered organization, a truly living collection.

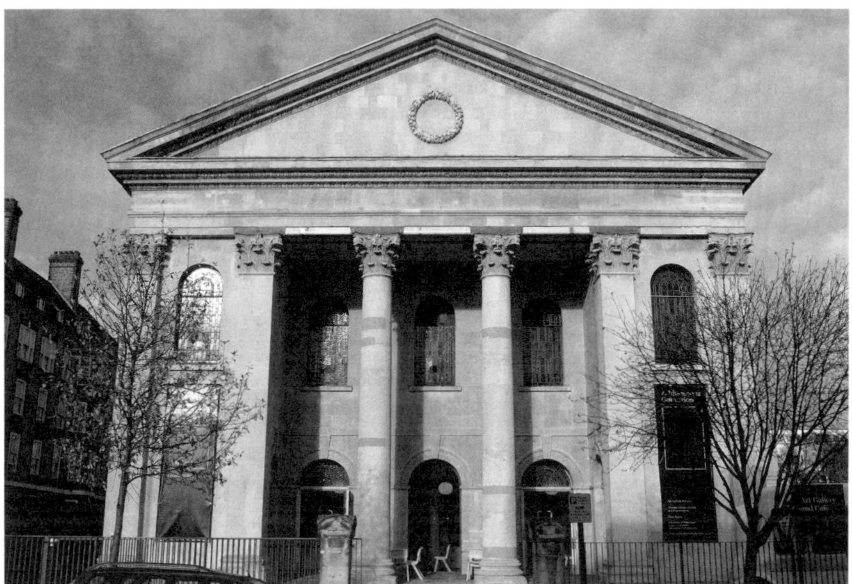

Zabludowicz Collection, London

What can a private museum do, that public institutions cannot?
How do you respond to people who criticize the proliferation of
private museums?

We have a great deal of flexibility in terms of how we
program. Visitor numbers are of course important to us, but
perhaps we have less pressure on us to generate blockbuster
shows. As a result we can be very responsive, working on
shorter timelines and with artists on more ambitious
projects, earlier in their careers, taking a few more risks
perhaps. We are also really focused on building long-term
relationships with artists, supporting their practices not
just through visibility in an exhibition, but also running
residencies, and of course through collecting their work and
committing to look after it in perpetuity. We see ourselves
as patrons in a very old-fashioned sense.

What are the greatest challenges in the long-term development of
a private museum? What are your plans for the next generation?

How we continue and build upon what we have achieved
in the future is a subject that greatly occupies our thoughts
at the moment. So much of what has happened evolved
organically, but as our children grow up we are able to talk
to them more about if and how they would like to be
involved in the collection. The greatest challenge as any
collector knows is about the long-term care of the artworks
we are fortunate enough to have. This will continue to be
the biggest question we address as we mature as a collection
and as a museum.

Do you have unrealized projects?

Oh there are so many! From major outdoor commissions to
exhibitions, to purchases that got away. We have many more
plans than we could ever realize. That is what keeps us
going!

1   A Grade II* listed buildings are "particularly important
buildings of more than special interest."

Jochen Zeitz
Zeitz MOCAA—Museum of Contemporary Art Africa, Cape Town

Jochen Zeitz founded the Zeitz Collection in 2002. He is also the cofounder and co-Chair of
The B Team, and founder of the Zeitz Foundation for intercultural ecosphere safety in 2008.
Having studied International Marketing and Finance he was CEO of PUMA until 2011.

Year of foundation: 2017
Size: Total area: 102,000 square feet (exhibition space: 65,000 square feet)
Number of employees: 56
Visitors: n/a

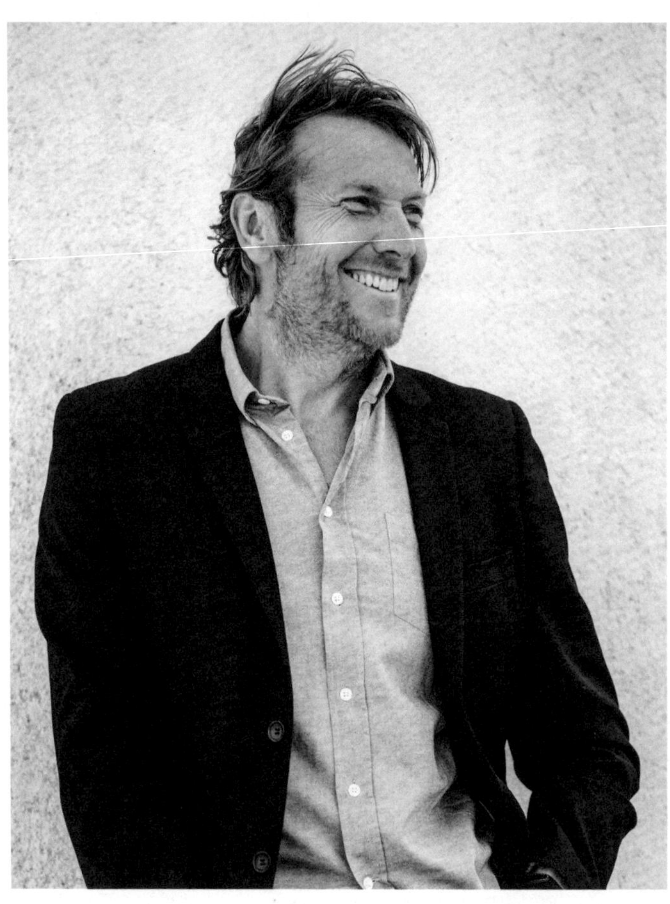

*What was your main motivation in
founding a museum?*

I love Africa and have had a home
in Kenya for many, many years,
so my passion for the continent
started decades ago. I bought some
art here and there, but only decided
to build a collection after I met
Mark Coetzee during the ground-
breaking show *30 Americans*—
one of the first major exhibitions
of African-American artists.
At the time, I was CEO of PUMA
and thanks to Marie-Claude Beaud,
who was an adviser at the time,
sponsored the show that Mark was
curating. I was just blown away by
the art. The show was such a success, it is still touring now, almost
ten years later, and totally ignited
my passion for contemporary
art from Africa and the diaspora.
    Mark and I really just shared
a vision for bringing African art to
the forefront of the contemporary
art world, and we both felt that
there was a need for a significant

cultural institution on the African continent that would focus on contemporary African art. After years of working together and looking for the right place for my growing collection, we then heard that the Victoria & Albert Waterfront was considering transforming the historic grain silo complex into a cultural institution/museum. All the stars seemed to align and it was the meeting of these two visions that ultimately resulted in the establishment of the partnership that has led us to Zeitz MOCAA–Museum of Contemporary Art Africa.

Did you have a specific model (i.e. an existing collection) in mind, and is there a tradition in your family of collecting art?

The amazing thing about collecting contemporary art from Africa is the pace at which it is evolving. This museum should feel like a living, breathing entity. Of course the collection contains many of the more established and well-known African artists, but many of the artists in the Zeitz MOCAA collection are incredibly young and their messages—whether they are personal, social, environmental, or political—are a powerful reflection on what is happening in Africa today. We believe the collection is cutting-edge and contemporary in the truest sense of the word. The collection was also built with a museum in mind, so the scale and scope of the artwork has always reflected that, and our mission has always been to create the most representative collection as possible. Africa is obviously vast, and it is our mission to represent its incredible diversity through art.

What is the focus of your collection? Do you concentrate on the presentation of your collection or on organizing temporary exhibitions?

The Zeitz Collection forms the founding collection of the museum. This has been specifically developed as a museum collection that takes into consideration issues of scale, relevance, representation, and archival responsibilities. We are continually striving to develop and improve the collection to ensure it best serves the interests of the museum.

How did you choose the location of the museum?

We saw the V&A Waterfront and Cape Town as the ideal
destination for Zeitz MOCAA. Cape Town has long been the
gateway to Africa for much of the world. This has created
a hugely diverse and creative city with a large number of
national and international visitors. The historic grain silo
building provides a fitting place to house such an important
cultural statement for Africa.

How did you choose the architect?

The architect was appointed by the V&A Waterfront, the
property owner and developer who have funded the redevelopment costs of the building, and we very much support
their selection of Thomas Heatherwick. The challenge they
faced with the grain silo complex was how to retain its
historic fabric, while also reimagining the interior space.
Thomas Heatherwick was able to demonstrate a sensitivity to
the industrial nature of the building, interpret the narrative
of the building, and provide a solution to the challenge of
the 42 silos. All these factors contributed to his appointment.
Heatherwick Studio is also working with three
South African architectural partners: Van Der Merwe
Miszewski Architects, Rick Brown Associates Architects,
and Jacobs Parker.

*How strongly are you involved in the running of the museum
(programming, management, etc.)?*

Both David Green [CEO of the V&A Waterfront] and I are
Co-Chairs of the Board of Trustees. Along with our Board,
we aim to ensure that Zeitz MOCAA acts in accordance
with its mission and constitution and to provide governance
and oversight of Zeitz MOCAA's activities to further the
objectives of the constitution. The curators and the curatorial programming are completely independent, and are based
on the museum's vision and mission.

Do you have an educational program?

There will be a strong educational strand to the work of
Zeitz MOCAA. Education is at the core of it. This is in addition
to our community outreach projects and engagement.

*What is your relationship with public or other institutions? Do you get
(public or private) funding?*

In addition to providing the museum with the collection
and the building, Zeitz MOCAA has been established with
working capital from its founders; however, the plan is
for the museum to become self-funding along with a broad
base of private supporters.

*In the past five years, what has been your greatest joy in running
the museum? And what has been the biggest challenge?*

I will tell you once we have opened the doors of the museum!

*What can a private museum do, that public institutions cannot?
And what do you reply to people who criticize the proliferation
of private museums?*

It's unrealistic to think you will not encounter criticism
during the life of any project and we will always engage with
constructive criticism. After all, we see this as a museum
for all of Africa—the only way we can ensure that this is
achieved, is by being as representative of the continent as
we can.

*What are the greatest challenges in the long-term development of
a private museum? And what are your plans for the next generation?*

We are constantly striving to remain as relevant as possible.
That is only possible through the diversity of the museum
in every respect.
    Looking further ahead, we want to continue to collect,
preserve, research, and exhibit cutting edge contemporary
art from Africa and its diaspora. We want to host international exhibitions, develop supporting educational and
enrichment programs for all, encourage intercultural
understanding, and guarantee access for all.

Do you have unrealized projects?

Always :-)

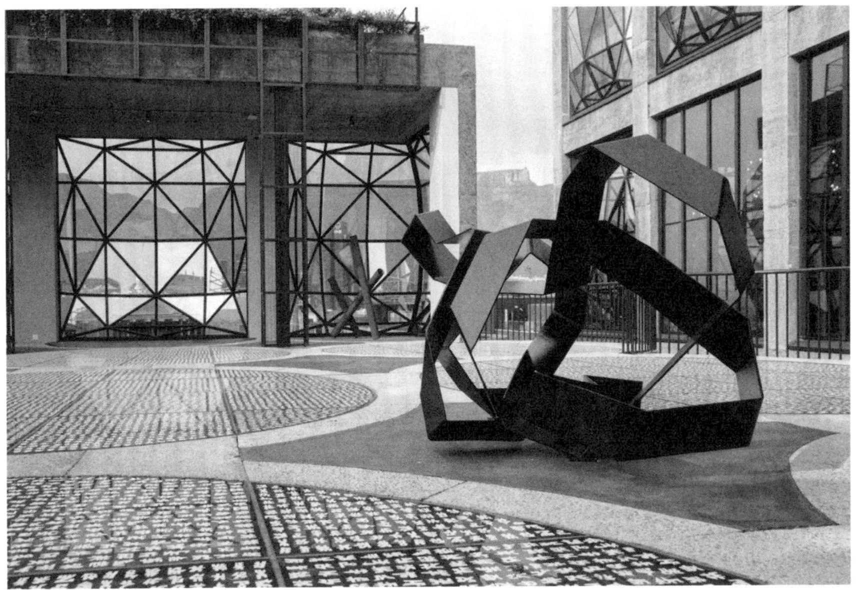

Sculpture Garden, Zeitz MOCAA–Museum of Contemporary Art Africa, Cape Town

AFTERWORD
Chris Dercon

*   Chris Dercon first started to comment on the rise of private museums in 2007. His original essay, "Indiana Jones and the Ruins of the Private Museum," was originally published in German on July 4, 2008, in the German newspaper *Süddeutsche Zeitung*. The text was later published in different languages and versions for publications in Germany, Great Britain, Spain, China, Switzerland, and France. This most recent, expanded, and updated version includes comments from private conversations with Sam Keller, Mark Wigley, and other specialists in the field.

Released in 2008, *Indiana Jones and the Kingdom of the Crystal Skull* continues the archeological quest for fiercely guarded treasures. In this, the fourth film of the popular series, Indiana Jones competes with Russians in pursuit of a crystal skull lost in the South American jungle. Damien Hirst's exhibition of his most recent works, entitled *Treasures from the Wreck of the Unbelievable* immediately recalls this plot. Hirst's show was on view in Venice in the summer of 2017, courtesy of industrialist and mega-collector François Pinault, owner of a luxury imperium, with a major share in Christie's auction house. Hirst's exhibition tells the story of a shipwreck supposedly discovered in the Indian Ocean. The ship contents were said to be the treasures of Amotan, a freed slave from Antioch, who spent his final days collecting artifacts from distant cultures. The ship that sank 2,000 years ago was recovered by divers, so the story goes, and its riches

were brought to Venice. In the Venice premises, owned
by Pinault, a number of the artifacts were exhibited "prior
to undergoing restoration." Damien Hirst recreated, so
to speak, Amaton's collection, a material and technical
endeavor that the world of contemporary art had hitherto
never seen. Moreover, the exhibition was meant by Hirst as
an homage to his supporter and collector Pinault. Architecture critic Niklas Maak wrote in the *Frankfurter Allgemeine
Sonntagszeitung*: "Two things are typical of this project:
the enjoyment of a certain super-affluent world of collectors
in presenting their own culture as a decadent park of ruins
(by which the damages that their own aggressive system
inflicts on this system become less obvious); and the ten-
dency to produce art objects that are as champagne-loaded,
golden, and shiny as the products by which these collectors
earn their money in real life … "[1] It is hard to envisage
an exhibition—in a private museum—that offers a more
pointed commentary on the present condition of the art
market and the art world in general.

Nevertheless, I venture to pitch another script in which
archeology and the commodification of globalized art
production are even more closely intertwined. I published it,
almost ten years ago, in *A Manual for the 21ˢᵗ-Century Art
Institution*, entitled "Indiana Jones and the Ruins of the
Private Museum."[2] Imagine this: the year is 2030 and the
still spritely explorer Indiana Jones hears rumors of a rich
American eccentric who has been forced to surrender his
huge estate, situated deep in the jungle territory of Costa
Rica, to a mysterious criminal gang. It is well known that
a privately owned museum of contemporary art once existed
within these abandoned grounds; however nature's lush
tropical vegetation has long since reclaimed the museum's
lavish structure, which was designed by a star architect.
All that remains is an impressive ruin, reminiscent of Hubert
Robert's sublime imaginary views of the Louvre. In among
the ruin, Jones discovers fragments of famous artworks
from the turn of the 21ˢᵗ century: a battered sculpture by
Jeff Koons, two weathered photographs by Andres Serrano,
a small mildewed painting by John Currin, and a decaying
live-size cartoon figure by Takashi Murakami. Indiana Jones
has been contracted by the Costa Rican government to escort

the artifacts to the San José Museum of Art, but rival salvage teams are lying in wait. The ensuing skirmishes are suddenly cut short when a huge earthquake tears open the ground, swallowing the art objects forever. United in the face of natural disaster, Jones and his rivals join forces to free two innocent holidaymakers, Jonathan Meese and his mother, who had been taken hostage by the mysterious criminal gang. To everyone's astonishment, it turns out that the gang leader, a key player in an international art insurance scam, is actually the owner of the abandoned museum and lost art collection.

Silly? Exaggerated? Yes, but only in part. Leading architects are currently designing eccentric private museums in far-flung locations across the globe. Yet often these private collections look much the same. With some exceptions, today's private museums for contemporary art are clones. Their contents are interchangeable, with the same artists and distinctly undifferentiated works. This is especially the case now that the phenomenon of the museum has spread on a global scale. Most of today's collections of art, both public and private, are understood as fragments of culture: a small selection from a greater whole. Each single piece in a museum has become a specimen, a piece of evidence. This has become even more evident with the rise of private museums, which in effect have become virtual spaces, belonging first and foremost to the world of the media, the glossy magazines, and design culture.

Like Indiana Jones, we realize that sooner or later most private museums cannot survive without state intervention. We only need to recall the fragility of private estates and crumbling institutions of the past, such as parks, castles, libraries, and collections. As Rem Koolhaas once exhorted, he and his colleagues should provide flexible, easily adapted designs for private museums, to reduce the financial burden on their heirs.[3] Cynical perhaps, yet sadly apt in this context: no matter how responsible a private collector is, the fact that this is a private setup with no long-term financial guarantee, let alone a consistent policy, means that this is a purely temporary state of affairs. A research project conceived by Columbia University's Graduate School of Architecture, Planning, and Preservation and the Deste Foundation for Contemporary Art stated that

we are presently witnessing a shift in the historical relationship between architecture and collecting practices that
inherited conceptions of the museum no longer adequately
describe. Indeed, in commenting on the report *Collecting
Architecture Territories*, commissioner Mark Wigley, in a recent
conversation with the author of this essay, quoted Dakis
Joannou of Deste, himself a renowned private collector,
saying that "most of the private museums do not know what
their future entails."[4]

Boris Groys views collecting as an art form in its own right
and argues that worthy examples such as the Barnes
Collection should be maintained with the help of public
funding. If an art collection is not of a high quality, then it
should not be preserved. Developments associated with
industrial and avant-garde production have fundamentally
changed the public nature of museums—and hence the
nature of private collections too.[5] The pressing question,
as Benjamin Buchloh points out, relates to the current role
of cultural producers in the formation of subjectivities.[6]
From the outset, the avant-garde was accompanied by a
constructive exchange between production, the figure of the
collector, and the collector's subjectivity. Over the course
of the 20th century this correlation changed beyond recognition. Market value became a key component of this dynamic.
And art came to be considered an investment over time.
Finally, when the artwork as an epiphany of a unique,
singular, subjective experience was destroyed, its symbolic
value, and therefore the expression of memory—no longer
intrinsic to the work—became displaced, giving way to the
production of pure spectacle. Consequently, many artists of
the late 20th century considered spectacularly situated venues
an important validation of their practice. The next stage in
this process is of course demonstrated by the extraordinary
proliferation of private museums, galleries, and "showrooms."
Perhaps in the future, neither complex layers of content,
nor a historical framework will be a necessary part of the
cultural practice or of artistic content. Moreover, there
is an expectation by insiders and outsiders alike that culture
can and will fulfill all the functions of consumption, thus
sustaining the role of cultural products. The rise of the
private museum is a perfect expression of this.

In contrast, the raison d'être of a public institution is to
ensure availability and visibility of public goods for many.
Its mission is to create an environment that makes
judgements for and by large audiences possible at all times.
One central feature of the history and essence of collecting
is the fact that private collectors make idiosyncratic choices:
they collect good as well as bad art. Accordingly, it is a
central responsibility of the guardians of public collections
to instruct the public and guide it in its assessment of works
of art. That means, first and foremost, drawing a distinction:
on the one hand there is the immensity of today's art
production—which evinces more and more parallels with
that of luxury goods—while on the other hand there are
artistic accomplishments that truly shape a culture. When
a private collector cooperates with a public museum, he
or she should trust that the public museum is a space where
culture is created. Many of today's private collectors can
afford purchases that are beyond the means of public
institutions. In contrast to many private collectors in today's
world, a public institution cannot forgo the production
of memory. Nor can we allow the formation of subjects to
metamorphose into an object-experience as a return on
investment. Public museums are the art-historical as well
as the social pharmakon, and not a supplement to the
private museum.

Indeed, in its structural internal plurality, the modern public
museum engenders an expanded cultural representation
that is much more than the possibilities of economics.
At least until recently, most visitors to public museums did
not perceive works of art as primarily commercial objects,
but rather as expressions of a cultured individual or of
a culture as a whole. It is the mission and duty of public
museums to help audiences to understand the objects
entrusted to them.

However that may be, we have to admit that the public
museum of today does not exist in a world of its own. It has
become one of many environments that comprise a much
wider museological project, because of the increasing
number of private museums and galleries, the huge rise
in private capital invested in art, and the ever decreasing

financial support from the state. The rise of the private
museum has become an inevitable reality, and not just
in those regions where public museums hardly exist or are
badly equipped. Often insiders need to remind us that
many of our grand public institutions began as very private
collections, or that most private collections will, in the end,
enter our public museums anyway. So why bother trying
to separate the two? Is there a happy end to it all? There
might be.

Nevertheless, it is important to note the differences
between private and public museums, and thus the—not
only, but central political—issues that are at stake. In China,
for instance, a few hundred private museums have been
created during the past decade, mainly due to new governmental policies, which have declared museum growth to
be part of the new economics, which created spin-offs such
as real estate deals between the state and corporations,
and an enormous growth of private wealth. Yet China is right
now facing the collapse of the private museum. Despite the
rapid growth in recent years, only a few have the capacity
to be sustainable. The dependency on single individuals only,
the anti-corruption efforts of the Chinese government,
censorship, along with developments in the Chinese art
market such as failing auction sales and the sagging Chinese
economy in general make these private museums fragile,
to say the least. However the best of Chinese contemporary
art can still only be seen in Chinese private museums.

In Italy, were it not for the colorful private
"Fondazioni," international, and even Italian contemporary
art would be totally absent and invisible for generations
because it is largely ignored by the majority of public
institutions, mainly due to the lack of funding. Confusion
abounds!

Not only at the level of countries is the function/role/status
of private museums varied and complex. Individual cities
also react very differently to private enterprises. Recently
the city of Geneva refused a huge private donation which
would have contributed to extending and renovating its
Musée d'art et d'histoire—the proposal was designed
by architect Jean Nouvel. In contrast, in other cities private
money speaks. The city of Arles cooperated fully with

Maja Hoffmann, a visionary international art patron, to erect an experimental building by Frank Gehry in order to show and produce the newest art, including complex experimental projects of immaterial art. Even if the city of Helsinki said no to yet another Guggenheim satellite, it wholeheartedly welcomed the private Amos Rex Art Museum, very much at the expense of the neighboring Kiasma museum. In Berlin we will soon witness the opening of many more private museums, which will outnumber public institutions of art.

The organizational structures of these and other private museums are becoming increasingly opaque as well as complex. Wim Pijbes, the former director of the famed Rijksmuseum in Amsterdam, was recently appointed director of the Museum Voorlinden, a private museum cum gardens in the wealthy Wassenaar suburb of The Hague. He resigned three months after the opening, explaining to the Dutch press that "there cannot be two captains on a ship." Meanwhile the Fondation Louis Vuitton, a private museum built on public land with special legal exemptions requiring the building to be gifted to the city of Paris after 55 years, propagandizes itself, with the moral support of the French government, as a perfect model of a "public institution" for today.

At least these, and other mega private museums such as Fondazione Prada in Milan or the future François Pinault Collection project at the former Stock Exchange in Paris, comment in "public" on their and our advantage of the temporality of their initiatives, and consequently their self-imposed, restricted longterm existence. As such we know what to expect.

The Zeitz MOCAA–Museum of Contemporary Art Africa in Cape Town is also announced as a public museum, but could only be realized through the large investments of a single private investor and collector.

And what about the arts center and botanic garden Instituto Inhotim, created by Bernardo Paz near Belo Horizonte in Minas Gerais, or the Museum of Old and New Art, the "hyper private museum" built and funded by David Walsh in Tasmania? Can a truly private endeavor offer more than a fickle phantasmagoria of a single individual? Time will tell. Bernardo Paz declared that, "Inhotim is now an international place, known in all continents and also known as a perspective for the future. All that translates as a spiritual state. And a spiritual state is something that doesn't end." But he also said, "We have started to decree, not for now, but for the next 30 years, the death of museums, which are like boxes buried in big cities."[7] To hijack Tim Schneider's excellent analysis of the recently opened Marciano Art Foundation in Los Angeles, these private art foundations cum museums offer "two templates for the private art foundation. One is a luxurious monument to concensus taste. The other is a movable feast, constantly reshaped by the distinct personality of the host."[8]

The current expansion of the "private museum" phenomenon can also be explained by the way in which some new pseudo-collectors and other risk-based benefactors (including many art dealers) are trying to gain more stature in order to ultimately increase their control over the art market.

Some private museums—whose architecture often reflects the ambitions of their founders—can be seen as the ultimate manifestations of the production of spectacle. Their operators have realized that a new cultural praxis may not necessarily need to rely on many years of experience or historically constructed memory. And how better to meet this objective than by transposing the model of cultural production into the context of "an architectural event"? Are the new private museums founded by artists such as Thomas Schütte to be considered the antidote?

Of course, there are some private collectors, like Nicoletta Fiorucci, who are openly reluctant to build their own museums, although they are increasingly rare. They are aware of the complexities of expanded investment, and the difficult conditions of such a long-term project. Instead, some collectors—such as Anthony d'Offay, Dimitris Daskalopoulos, Harald Falckenberg, Ingvild Goetz, Thomas Borgmann, and Uli Sigg—seek to create partnerships with the public sector. And public museums recognize the benefits of exploring these forms of public-private partnership.

Finally, to complicate the situation a little more, the private museum often takes on the role of the failing public cultural sector in cities and regions, where public museums are absent. I refer to recent initiatives in Amman, Beirut,

Chiang Mai, New Delhi, Istanbul, and Jeddah in which individuals and private organizations create private museums in the absence of, or as an alternative to, a government cultural axis. This model, even when considered with all the usual precautions, is an example that seems to take the production of memory seriously.

But, many new and inexperienced collectors seem particularly reluctant to accept (and this is an effect of the art market and global capital flows) that owning contemporary art is, for the most part, a long-term investment, bringing little or no short-term gain. Moreover, collectors are beginning to understand that the functioning of their own systems grounded in capitalism and the pragmatic approach to the economic parameters that some of them employ (such as profitability, efficiency of costs, short-term actions and strategies, endless accumulation, and expansion of a directionless diversity, discretion about information regarding their assets and costs) amount to pale imitations of the public museum.

The private sector almost always adheres to widely differing priorities from those of public institutions. It often prefers the production of cultural industry, which, rather than aspiring to sustainability, is characterized by short-term horizons and short-term resources, specialization, and fads. This production is governed by subjective and economic decisions that ultimately lead to more fragmentation, but also to a lack of quality in artistic production. Artists produce more on request, while art criticism has become a kind of creation ex nihilo.

There is another corresponding paradox: as there are more private capital owners who invest in art, many more "serious" collectors, as they often call themselves, such as Christian Boros, Axel Haubrok, Erika and Rolf Hoffmann, Thomas Olbricht, and Julia Stoschek all in Berlin, or Anton and Annick Herbert in Ghent, increasingly desire and deserve public or critical recognition of what they do. At the same time, these collections are among the most adventurous and personal in the world, without being whimsical. I would add here the initiatives of TBA21 formerly in Vienna, Lafayette Anticipations–Fondation d'entreprise Galeries Lafayette in Paris, the Garage Museum in Moscow.

These private museums, with the Fondazione Prada in Milan and Venice taking the lead, clearly understand that a push for the interdisciplinary is yielding both innovative building types and new exhibition formats, in favor of spaces and projects that bring people together.

In this context it is interesting to mention an open letter that pioneering collector Anton Herbert recently published, referring to a conversation about the future of private and public collections in Flanders and the Netherlands: "The concern to give a future to a collection is admittedly a most difficult task for the private collector. In this challenge lies the factor of publicness. The chances for success are utopian and very limited. The private collection that goes public at a later moment in time has to make clear its very characteristics of subjectivity, flexibility, selectivity, quality, and independence. These essentials have to be built in before. That is: before the work that is necessary to make the collection public. Many excellent private collections of earlier generations are lost. What is the reason behind this?"[9]

It is indeed interesting to note that currently many collectors, not only of Swiss origin, are knocking on Sam Keller's door, asking how to be part of the Fondation Beyeler's successful operations in a private-public environment, as if looking for a role model, and possibly salvation. But, according to Keller, most of these requests barely understand the consequences and necessities of a private collection going public.

On the other hand, painter Kerry James Marshall stated in a public conversation that unless Beyoncé and her colleagues started to invest in American museums, the future for African-American art looks bleak: "We don't have an independent economic apparatus that generates the kind of money that museums, art galleries, collectors have that helps make the art world run. We don't have control of an apparatus that can generate the same kind of money and the resources that already exist in what people call the mainstream."[10]

It is time to establish new standards for cooperation between private collectors and public museums. These relationships cannot be based only on gratitude and good faith. The collector who works with a public museum must accept the museum as a place of symbolic value—in the long term—for art. The museums should only approach private collectors who share this conviction. The public museum should cater to the private collector, who not only supports the arts and artists, but who also strengthens the broader culture of public museums. It is this combination of efforts that produces culture.

The recent project *Sheffield: Going Public* is a constructive, future orientated example of the above. The project, conceived by international private collectors and museums in Sheffield, was set up to explore how public galleries and philanthropists can better develop meaningful, beneficial relationships. The strong message, endorsed by influential collectors such as Nicolas Cattelain, Jack Kirkland, Valeria Napoleone, and Patrizia Sandretto Re Rebaudengo, was that philanthropists want to feel that they are in an active, stimulating, and progressive partnership with the institutions they support.

I want to emphasize that cooperation between public museums and private collectors is fundamentally healthy and constructive. There have been—and still are—many private collectors to whom we are grateful. Nevertheless, we must accept that a division exists between the interests of some private collectors and public museums, between collecting and educating, between the different practices in art, and different practices in museology.

Just as object-based art is rooted in a world of material production and manufacture, so the increasingly experiential art of today echoes our new, immaterial social systems and economic networks. We must accept that this will change the future of public and private collections alike, and thus of public and private museums.

The question concerning the future of the museum arises more urgently today than ever. Now that the new Tate Modern has opened, many people want to know how the museum will be able to host all possible disciplines, ranging from fine arts to film, performance, dance, and music under one roof. What boundaries still exist? Will these boundaries also cease to exist in the case of the private museums of the future?

[1] Niklas Maak, "Trans Europa Express," in *Frankfurter Allgemeine Sonntagszeitung*, May 14, 2017.

[2] Chris Dercon, "Indiana Jones and the Ruins of the Private Museum," in Shamita Sharmacharja (ed.), *A Manual for the 21ˢᵗ Century Art Institution*, Walter König, London 2009, p. 110–117.

[3] He adds: "There is another interesting scenario, which is to use the empty part of the museum as a repository for the collections of the future abandoned private museums of current private collectors. A kind of preventive preservation anticipating the tragic situation wherein the children of collectors at some point stop sharing the same respect and affinity for the works as their parents, and either want to sell or no longer maintain the very expensive spaces." Rem Koolhaas, Jacques Herzog, Mark Wigley, "Haus der Kunst: Built Ideology," in *032c*, Berlin, Summer 2008, p. 68. https://032c.com/2008/built-ideology-haus-der-kunst (last accessed May 2018).

[4] Craig Buckley, Mark Wasiuta (eds.), *Collecting Architecture Territories*, Columbia University's Graduate School of Architecture Planning, and Preservation and Deste Foundation for Contemporary Art, New York 2014.

[5] Boris Groys, "Die Logik der Sammlung/Sammler versus Museum," in *Kritik* 2, 1995, p. 45.

[6] In Sabine Breitwieser (ed.), *Sammlung Archiv Kommunikation*, Generali Foundation, Vienna 1999, p. 45–56.

[7] Gisele Regatao, "Considering Art and Crisis in Brazil, from Tropicália to Today," *Hyperallergic*, October 10, 2016. https://hyperallergic.com/329087/considering-art-crisis-brazil-tropicalia-today last accessed May 2018).

[8] Tim Schneider, "Why the Marciano Foundation Embodies the Existential Crisis Facing All Private Museums," artnet.com, May 24, 2017. https://news.artnet.com/market/new-marciano-foundation-existential-crisis-private-museums-everywhere-971639 (last accessed May 2018).

[9] Herbert Collection, "De privatisering van het kunstenveld," *De Witte Raaf*, 187, May–June 2017, p. 5.

[10] "Kerry James Marshall and the Invisible Man," *032c*, May 9, 2017. https://032c.com/kerry-james-marshall (last accessed May 2018).

Imprint

EDITED BY
Cristina Bechtler and Dora Imhof

EDITING
Barbara Biedermann, Clément Dirié, and Dora Imhof

EDITORIAL COORDINATION
Patricia Mosquera

COPY EDITING AND PROOFREADING
Clare Manchester

DESIGN CONCEPT
Gavillet & Cie, Geneva

DESIGN
Nicolas Eigenheer, Nicolas Leuba

PRINT AND BINDING
Musumeci S.p.A., Quart (Aosta)

TYPEFACE
Genath (www.optimo.ch)

PHOTO CREDITS
All the images reproduced are courtesy of the interviewees'
foundations and museums.

Ziba Ardalan: Jake Gavin (18), Jack Hems/2016 (27t),
Benjamin Westoby/2017 (27b); Christian Boros: Magnus Reed
(28), NOSHE (33); Eli and Edythe Broad: The Broad
Foundation (34), Benny Chan (39); Gil Bronner: Albrecht
Fuchs (40), Stefan Müller (45); Dimitris Daskalopoulos:
Marco Anelli/2016 (46), Panos Kokkinias/2015 (51); Jens
Faurschou: Anders Sune Berg (52), Jonathan Leijonhufvud/
2015 (57); Soichiro Fukutake: Courtesy of Soichiro Fukutake
(58), Fujitsuka Mitsumasa (65t), Ken'ichi Suzuki (65b);
Ingvild Goetz: Gerald von Foris/2012–2013 (66), Wilfried
Petzi/2011 & Architects: ©Herzog & de Meuron, Basel (71);

Dakis Joannou: Alexia Antsakl (72), Hugo Glendinning (75);
Grażyna Kulczyk: Adam Pluciński (78), Courtesy of the
architects Lukas Voellmy and Chasper Schmidlin, Zurich (85);
Savina Lee: Courtesy of Savina Lee (86, 89); Eugenio López
Alonso: Jean-Philippe Michel (92, 97); Philippe Méaille:
Courtesy of Philippe Méaille (98, 103); Leonid Mikhelson:
Sergey Sapozhnikov (104), Renzo Piano Building Workshop
(109); Judith Neilson: Courtesy of White Rabbit (112, 117);
Bernardo Paz: Daniela Paoliello & Rossana Magri (118),
Eduardo Eckenfels (121); Lekha Poddar: Courtesy of Lekha
Poddar (126); Nadia Samdani: Courtesy of Nadia Samdani
(130), Noor Photoface (137); Patrizia Sandretto Re
Rebaudengo: Alessandro Albert (140), Maurizio Elia (149);
Mario Saradar: Courtesy of Mario Saradar (152); Bernar
Venet: Steve Benisty (158), Jérôme Cavalière. Courtesy
Archives Bernar Venet, New York (163); Lu Xun: Courtesy
of Lu Xun (166, 171); Anita Zabludowicz: David Bebber (172),
Thierry Bal (177); Jochen Zeitz: Antonia Steyn/Zeitz
MOCAA (180, 185)

Printed in Europe

PUBLISHED BY
JRP | Ringier
Limmatstrasse 270
CH–8005 Zurich
T +41 43 311 27 50
E info@jrp-ringier.com
www.jrp-ringier.com

IN CO-EDITION WITH
Les presses du réel
35, rue Colson
F–21000 Dijon
T +33 3 80 30 75 23
E info@lespressesdureel.com
www.lespressesdureel.com

ISBN 978-3-03764-520-8 (JRP | Ringier)
ISBN 978-2-84066-983-8 (Les presses du réel)

Distribution

JRP | Ringier publications are available internationally
at selected bookstores and from the following distribution
partners:

GERMANY AND AUSTRIA
Vice Versa Distribution GmbH
www.viceversaartbooks.com

FRANCE
Les presses du réel
www.lespressesdureel.com

SWITZERLAND
AVA Verlagsauslieferung AG
www.ava.ch

UK AND OTHER EUROPEAN COUNTRIES
Cornerhouse Publications HOME
www.cornerhousepublications.org

USA, CANADA, ASIA, AND AUSTRALIA
ARTBOOK | D. A. P.
www.artbook.com

For a list of our partner bookshops or for any general
questions, please contact JRP | Ringier directly at
info@jrp-ringier.com, or visit our homepage
www.jrp-ringier.com for further information.

Documents Series 27:
Cristina Bechtler and
Dora Imhof [ed.]
The Private Museum of the Future

This book is the twenty-seventh
volume in the "Documents" series,
dedicated to critics' writings.

The series was founded by
Lionel Bovier and Xavier Douroux.

Also available

DOCUMENTS SERIES (IN ENGLISH)

John Baldessari, *More Than You Wanted to Know
About John Baldessari*
ISBN 978-3-03764-192-7 (JRP|Ringier) [*Vol. 1*]
ISBN 978-3-03764-256-6 (JRP|Ringier) [*Vol. 2*]

Cristina Bechtler & Dora Imhof, *Museum of the Future*
ISBN 978-3-03764-383-9 (JRP|Ringier)
ISBN 978-2-84066-759-9 (Les presses du réel)

Sarah Burkhalter & Laurence Schmidlin, *Spacescapes.
Dance & Drawing since 1962*
ISBN 978-3-03764-469-0 (JRP|Ringier)
ISBN 978-2-84066-917-3 (Les presses du réel)

Gabriele Detterer & Maurizio Nannucci, *Artist-Run Spaces*
ISBN 978-3-03764-191-0 (JRP|Ringier)
ISBN 978-2-84066-512-0 (Les presses du réel)

Tim Griffin, *Writings on Wade Guyton*
ISBN 978-3-03764-473-7 (JRP|Ringier)
ISBN 978-2-84066-945-6 (Les presses du réel)

Hans Ulrich Obrist, *A Brief History of Curating*
ISBN 978-3-905829-55-6 (JRP|Ringier)
ISBN 978-2-84066-287-7 (Les presses du réel)

Tomáš Pospiszyl, *An Associative Art History*
ISBN 978-3-03764-517-8 (JRP|Ringier)
ISBN 978-2-84066-982-1 (Les presses du réel)

Alice Rawsthorn, *Design as an Attitude*
ISBN 978-3-03764-521-5 (JRP|Ringier)
ISBN 978-2-84066-984-5 (Les presses du réel)